# DRIVEN *by* Eternity

MAKING YOUR LIFE COUNT TODAY *&* FOREVER

*Workbook and Devotional*

# JOHN BEVERE

Project Management and Consulting: **www.vaughnstreet.com**

ISBN 1-933185-03-1

Requests for information should be addressed to:
Messenger International
P. O. Box 888, Palmer Lake, CO 80133-0888
www.messengerintl.org

*COVER, INTERIOR DESIGN & PRINTING:*
Eastco Multi Media Solutions, Inc
3646 California Rd.
Orchard Park, NY 14127
**www.eastcomultimedia.com**

Writer: Holt Vaughn
Editor: Deborah Moss
Design Manager: Aaron La Porta
Designers: Heather Wierowski, Aaron La Porta

Printed in the United States of America

# Table of Contents

# A Personal Message
## from John to the Students

I'd like to welcome you to *Driven by Eternity*. I, along with our team at Messenger International, have spent hundreds of hours in prayer, writing, and teaching to bring this prophetic message to you. I'm so happy you have chosen to walk through it with us. Every book I have written has profoundly touched my life; however, none have touched my life as much as this one.

The truths contained in this book and workbook are so needed as we seek to be kingdom people who live for the eternal, not for self. When we have an eternal perspective, we will pursue and make decisions differently. We will endure things we would otherwise yield to. Our whole life takes a different perspective. The world lives for the day; however, true believers are motivated by the everlasting and will be rewarded eternally for it.

When God began to deal with me about penning this message, I wrestled with how to communicate eternal judgments and rewards to a generation that has heard very little on this foundational doctrine of Christianity. The Holy Spirit whispered, "Tell them a story, as Jesus did, and teach around it." I expected to write only three to five pages, but the allegory continued to unfold until it turned into one-fourth of the book.

Because the truth presented in the book revolves around this allegory, it is crucial that you read or hear it before you enter into the second hour of this workbook. You can do it one of two ways. First, you can read chapters two, three, and eight of the book *Driven by Eternity*, or second, you can hear it in our audio drama entitled *Affabel*, which we professionally produced in Hollywood. I personally hope you will do both.

This curriculum will take you to a place where you can actually live the reality of a transformed life – a life of passion, glory, and power! A life that counts now and forever is available to each of us! More than just knowing about God and what He does, you can actually know God and who He is, and you can learn how to live in a way that brings rewards for you in heaven! You will be transformed by the renewing of your heart and mind and in the way you think and live. You can carry His grace and glory to multitudes of others.

Let's join together and begin right now on this eternal quest! You will find the Word of God, the life of the Father, and the presence of the Holy Spirit to be the most energizing, exhilarating, and transforming experience you have ever known! And you will see how you can influence others for eternity as well!

# DRIVEN *by* Eternity

You have an incredible resource in your hands: A combined devotional/journal and workbook based on John Bevere's book *Driven By Eternity*!
Full of:

- meaningful and memorable quotations
- deeply moving biographical and historical sketches
- thought provoking, life-transforming questions
- "Hot Topics" for discussion
- Scriptures to live by

this study makes for a one-of-a-kind and riveting encounter with God!

## *Devotional:*
### Easy-to-Use Instructions for Students

Growing in your relationship with the Lord is about developing your passion, love, humility, and obedience. You can use the devotional on its own but it is best if you use it along with the book *Driven By Eternity* and its video teachings.

Here are some detailed easy-to-use instructions:

- **There are twelve video sessions and twelve weeks of devotions and journaling.** Each week of the devotional journal is designed to take what you learn in the book and the videos and bring it to reality as you spend time with God.

- **There are also three chapters in the workbook that are based on the allegories (chapters 2, 3 & 8) from the book *Driven By Eternity*.** There are no video sessions about these three workbook chapters, so use the book for your answers. There is also a Hollywood produced audio drama available, *Affabel: Window of Eternity*, on Compact Disc which brings these chapters to life in a powerful way. See page 279 for info on ordering.

- **This is your personal time, and it can be as flexible as you need it to be.** You may want to go through it as your daily time with God, but you don't have to. This is set up as a 12-week encounter. You could start each morning or finish each evening with the devotional.

- **The key is consistency.** Choose the schedule you'll follow, and then keep it faithfully. Life is full of changing circumstances, so if you miss some of your scheduled times, that's OK. Just get back to it; pick up where you left off, and follow through to completion. You will be rewarded in eternity for the faithfulness you give in devotion to the Lord.

- **Set aside your quiet time,** preferably in a place where you and God can be together, uninterrupted.

# Workbook:
## Easy-to-Use Instructions for Students

## Easy-to-Use Student Instructions...

- Begin by reading the book *Driven By Eternity*. Don't be afraid to under line or write in the book. Be prayerful, and keep your Bible handy as you read. As you go, remember to make notes and mark pages for any questions you may have.

- There are twelve video sessions, each of which corresponds to a chapter in the workbook and book.

- The answers to the questions are taken from the book and the videos.

- A complete transcript of each video session is available by contacting Messenger International at US (toll free) 1-800-648-1477, Australia 1-300-650-577, or UK 44 (0) 870-745-5790.

- There are also three chapters in the workbook that are based on the allegories (chapters 2, 3 & 8) from the book *Driven By Eternity*. There are no video sessions about these three workbook chapters, so use the book for your answers. There is also a Hollywood produced audio drama available, *Affabel: Window of Eternity*, on Compact Disc which brings these chapters to life in a powerful way. See page 279 for info on ordering.

## Group Study...

- Before each group session, find out how your group leader wants to organize the sessions. You may be asked to complete the video and workbook chapter before each session. Others may prefer that you wait until the group meets to do the workbook questions. Follow the instructions your group leader gives you, as this is only a guide.

- As you watch the video with the group, use the spaces provided for answers.

- Enjoy the video. You don't have to keep up with all the questions and answers.

- During each session, your group leader will provide answers and facilitate discussions. Whether you are a "people" person or more reserved, you will get much more out of this message if you pray and ask the Holy Spirit to lead you as an active participant. Prayer is essential to your life in Christ, so spend quality time with the Lord before you come to each session.

• There will be times for prayer and ministry throughout the sessions. Go to each session expectant that the Lord will move!

## Personal Study...

• If you have purchased this curriculum and are not part of a group, simply watch each video session with your workbook open. You can watch one time through and take notes, and then go back and fill in all the answers while referring to the video, or you can pause the video and fill in the answers as you go.

## Journaling...

One of the features of this study is that it includes times of "journaling" or recording thoughts, prayers and feelings in some of the sessions. This may be new to you. Webster's dictionary defines journaling as "a record of experiences, ideas, or reflections kept regularly for private use." In the Old Testament, God told His people to write things down, so they could be passed down from generation to generation. Of course, we have the New Testament for the simple reason that it was written down as a record of the words and works of Jesus and His disciples. We are to keep His words written upon our hearts, and journaling is an excellent way to accomplish this.

The following are not all hard and fast rules, but they are helpful suggestions for the journaling portions:

• Always record the date and time.

• Follow the instructions for each particular journaling portion. Record feelings: good, bad, or indifferent.

• Make note of thoughts and images that the Holy Spirit brings before you and write down Bible verses that come alive to you.

• Write what God tells and reveals to you, even if you do not fully understand it.

You'll quickly find that as God teaches you about eternity, He will start speaking to you more than ever before!

Journaling can be an invaluable tool for years to come. Journaling will help you understand how God is working in your life as you see your progress and gain clarity in your walk with God. You will be able to look back and see the amazing works God has accomplished in your life as you've grown in intimacy with Him. It will be a great source of inspiration and faith to keep your heart on fire for God. It will be a way to enable you to share with others the wonderful testimony of what God has done in your life.

**To complete the Kingdom of Affabel sections on pages: 21, 25 and 119, please refer to the *Driven by Eternity* book or the audio drama, *Affabel*.**

AN EPIC AUDIO DRAMA FROM *DRIVEN BY ETERNITY*

# AFFABEL
### WINDOW OF ETERNITY

*Awaken* YOUR *Soul* WITH THIS *Epic* OF ANOTHER *Time & Place...*

THIS HOLLYWOOD PRODUCED AUDIO DRAMA IS A CAPTIVATING ALLEGORY FROM JOHN'S BOOK

DRIVEN *by* Eternity

4 CD SET

JOHN BEVERE

*Packaging design subject to change.*

See page 279 for ordering information and a money saving coupon.

The Eternal

# HOUR 1

Please refer to Chapter 1,

The Eternal,

in the *Driven by Eternity* book

and video session 1.

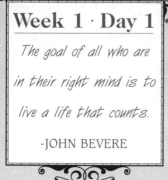

## Week 1 · Day 1

*The goal of all who are in their right mind is to live a life that counts.*

-JOHN BEVERE

Life is full of things we have no power to control. Time's passing is at the top of that list. No matter who we are, how much we possess, what we do, or where we live, we are all subject to it. Moments turn into minutes, hours, and then days. Days become weeks, which blend into years, and then fold into ages gone by. We may work hard to "manage" this, but that is all we can do. Many will admit that even basic time management is a moment-by-moment effort if not a pull-your-hair-out struggle.

Quietly, raucously, joyfully, or violently, time relentlessly progresses. We experience it collectively (think about standing with dozens of people in a long waiting line) and personally (ask a pregnant woman who is about to give birth – having that baby is seriously about the passing of time, and it is intensely personal!).

In the end – whether at work or play, whether sick or healthy, whether young or old – we face time. In groups or one on one, time waits for nobody and yields to nothing. It is seemingly merciless. Tyrannical. All powerful in its advance. Hopelessly unbending, it begs a question and screams its warning to all people: *How are you going to respond to time? What are you going to do about its passing? How are you living and dealing with every moment of your life, which before you blink or think is forever lost?*

Let the psalmist of old teach you life's secret today: *we should be getting while the getting is good!*

But I pray to you, O LORD, *in the time of your favor*; in your great love, O God, answer me with your sure salvation.

-PSALM 69:13, NIV, EMPHASIS ADDED

Now is the time to act – while God has favored you with breath in your lungs and a sound mind! What should you do about time? First and foremost settle the supreme issue: **what you make of time depends on your response to the Ruler of time.**

The wise shall inherit glory, but shame shall be the legacy of fools.

-PROVERBS 3:35

Listen to my instruction and be wise; do not ignore it.

-PROVERBS 8:33, NIV

Pray, and He will answer. Do it now when the time of His favor is upon you.

*God, I come to you in the name of Jesus, Your Son. He died for me and my sins. You raised Him from the dead. He is at your right hand now in heaven. Lord, You who are the maker and ruler of time, please come strongly into my life and teach me to make my life count today and forever. I want to inherit glory. I want to be wise with Your wisdom. I want a legacy with true meaning. I will not ignore You, Lord. I have heard the call to follow You, and by Your Holy Spirit I will persevere and make the most of my time for now and for eternity.*

What a glorious gift is His Word to you right now. It will have eternal value. Take some time to thank and praise God for the Scriptures! Then think for a moment about your prayer and this devotion. Record the most important thoughts of your time today.

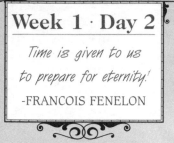

## Week 1 · Day 2

*Time is given to us
to prepare for eternity!*

-FRANCOIS FENELON

Time's passing is deeply interwoven with another of life's inevitabilities. In time, death will come to us all. Nothing is more assuredly approaching. And nothing could be more fiercely personal. Soldiers may share deathly battles in wartimes, but each warrior ultimately faces that moment supremely alone. Families may gather in peaceful warmth at death's bedside, but relatives and friends cannot take the place of their beloved. It is for each of us alone to finally answer to time and its natural conclusion, death.

So why is it so few talk openly about death, let alone prepare for it? More than half of the citizens of the United States of America – wealthy, educated, and technically advanced – do not even have a last will and testament.[2] It may cause an uproar to talk religion or politics with friends or family, but if you really want to see things get crazy, just try to get close to the subject of death. All over the world people run from it, fear it, and generally are profoundly unprepared for it, even if some (the terminally ill, the death-row inmate) have time to know it is soon coming.

Oh, but there is blissful news! It need not be this way. Time is a gift given to us by its master, God. And because of the Lord Jesus Christ, we can use our time, not to lament its passing, but to prepare for a glorious homecoming. Christ went to prepare a place for us, His believers, and then sent the Holy Spirit to live in us. If we lead a life of graceful obedience to God, we are prepared and can eagerly look forward to the time when God calls us to Himself, no matter the circumstances.

"In My Father's house are many mansions; if it were not so, I would have told you. I go to prepare a place for you. And if I go and prepare a place for you, I will come again and receive you to Myself; that where I am, there you may be also. And where I go you know, and the way you know."

Thomas said to Him, "Lord, we do not know where You are going, and how can we know the way?"

Jesus said to him, "I am the way, the truth, and the life."

-JOHN 14:2-6

What a revelation for us! Jesus shows His mastery of time as He declares He has gone before us for the very purpose of preparing a place for us in eternity! He also clearly tells us we know where He is going and the way to get there.

**Knowing this, everything changes!** Rather than living a lifetime of denial, suppression, fear, or ignorance, you can live life as God intended. Time was given to prepare you for death itself and more importantly for what happens after you die, when endless time will either be your greatest blessing – or a most tormenting curse.

Pray. Think upon these things. Are you using the gift of time to prepare for eternity?

1. Francois Fenelon, *Meditations on the Heart of God*, Christian Classics (Orleans, MA: Paraclete Press, 1997), chapter 36, "Time Is Precious."
2. "Most Americans Still Don't Have a Will," a survey conducted by the legal Web site FindLaw in August 2002, found that only 44.4 percent of American adults currently have a will; 53.3 percent said they do not have a will, while 2.2 percent did not know or had no response. http://www.moreinformationplease.com/ss.l!GUID~16E94353242E71CC54659D90E2EF964A (accessed January 3, 2006).

# Week 1 · Day 3

*Wisdom gives us the knowledge and ability to make right choices at the opportune time. Wisdom is not just for the mentally sharp; it is for all who fear the Lord and are found in Christ.*

-JOHN BEVERE

In our last devotion we saw that God has given us time as a gift to prepare for all of eternity. This is a genuine change of thinking for most people. What should your response be to this?

You can be happy to know a simple response is enough. Notice that the word is *simple*, not *easy*. The difference between those is important. It is as simple as following Jesus one day at a time, one circumstance at a time, moment by moment. To the best of your ability, in divine combination with His abilities – through the Holy Spirit in you – you live out His words, His principles, His love, His truth.

Another way to put it would be this: you follow Him daily as you live a life of graceful obedience by the power of the Holy Spirit inside you. You make Scripture-based, Holy Spirit-led choices. Living life according to His ways, not yours, is the key. Choosing obedience over sin, Christ over self, life over death, you make a pilgrim's progress along the path to eternity.

It may not always be easy. Times may get very difficult, but it is always as elementary as following the Master. Face life and times in His power and with His Word, and you fall into the coveted category of the wise. No matter how intelligent, cultured, or educated you are (or aren't) and not based on your financial or social standings. Wisdom is for the followers of Christ: a gift for the asking, a blessing for the obedient.

How do we find our way to a life that really matters, now and forever? How do we get to heaven's eternal glories? **If you follow Him, you end up where He is.**

If anyone serves Me, let him follow Me; and where I am, there My servant will be also. If anyone serves Me, him My Father will honor.

-JOHN 12:26

Pray today about the choices you are making in life. Are they in line with God's truth? Are they taking you toward eternal things or temporary pleasures? It is of paramount importance that we make the correct choices in how we live our daily lives. Remember, James 1:5 says that if anyone asks God for wisdom, He will give it freely.

## Week 1 · Day 4

*...a continual looking forward to the eternal world is not (as some modern people think) a form of escapism or wishful thinking, but one of the things a Christian is meant to do. It does not mean that we are to leave the present world as it is. If you read history you will find that the Christians who did the most for the present world were just those who thought most of the next!*

-C. S. LEWIS

A believer's faith is neither escapism nor a crutch. It is a way of life, or at least it is supposed to be. The skeptic or agnostic who believes it is not possible to know that there is a god – or the atheist who denies the very existence of God – also makes faith a way of life. And it is indeed faith if you define it as allegiance to or confidence in the value or trustworthiness of an idea. So skeptics, agnostics, and atheists have their faith and Christians have theirs as well. Besides the fact that our faith is in a Person, what is the difference in the ideas?

This brings us back to the "at least it is supposed to be" fragment above in our first sentence. A follower of Jesus Christ should *look* like a follower of Jesus.

> He who says, "I know Him," and does not keep His commandments, is a liar, and the truth is not in him.
>
> -1 JOHN 2:4

**No matter where you go in today's world, if you truly are practicing what you preach, you will stand out among the crowd.** You will look different from the rest of the folks around you. Look at the words of Jesus in Matthew 7:19-21:

> Every tree that does not bear good fruit is cut down and thrown into the fire. Therefore by their fruits you will know them. Not everyone who says to Me, "Lord, Lord," shall enter the kingdom of heaven, but he who does the will of My Father in heaven.

And read what the apostle Paul wrote to the church at Colossi:

> And we pray this in order that you may live a life worthy of the Lord and may please him in every way: bearing fruit in every good work, growing in the knowledge of God.
>
> -COLOSSIANS 1:10, NIV

As you live your life in such a way that those around you – especially in difficult situations – see that you act and react differently, biblically, and with supernatural integrity, hope, and courage; you will leave an indelible mark on history. Your name doesn't have to end up in the encyclopedias to have had eternal impact on the world! But your heart and mind will have to be daily fixed on eternal things.

Focus today's prayer on the truths in our three Scripture verses above. Recite them aloud, and meditate on God's Word to you. Write down things in your life that need to change as well as any encouraging words.

1. C. S. Lewis, *Mere Christianity* (San Francisco: HarperSanFrancisco, 2001), 134.

# Week 1 · Day 5

*It is since Christians have largely ceased to think of the other world that they have become so ineffective in this. Aim at Heaven and you will get earth "thrown in": aim at earth and you will get neither.*

-C. S. LEWIS

You've probably heard the saying: "They're so heavenly minded they're no earthly good." Like any adage, this came about because it may indeed have an element of truth to it. There are some who in the name of heaven are so lost in themselves or caught up in wrong thinking and things that they are flighty, unstable, or even irresponsible.

But it can be a slam against a great principle as well. History is full of people who wanted to do something beyond them, something requiring supernatural assistance, something "engraved in stone" that would last. It's no secret that the Johann Gutenbergs, Martin Luthers, Winston Churchills and Leonardo da Vincis of the world were caught up body, mind, and spirit in something bigger than themselves. Some even looked to be no earthly good at times.

Creating a company that changes the entire business world is one thing. Inventing amazing things is another, ruling nations another; and pleasing God is yet another. There are "elements" of God in all as He is sovereign ruler, omnipotent, omniscient, and omnipresent. Nothing good happens without His hand upon it. That is good news – wondrous news – for all mankind.

But what does all this mean, practically speaking? It means you are a valuable asset to the world right now because you can change things around you by the power and wisdom of God. Seemingly tiny little things that you can do make all the eternal difference, simply because you are bearing God's fruit!

Take your neighbors a meal when they need it, or shovel their sidewalk and hand them a good Bible-based book you picked out just for them. Maybe you are a pastor or have a business. Regardless of your daily calling, your life is that of a vessel of God. You carry eternity in your heart and hands. **People are just waiting for you to think of them, pray for them, give to them, and reach them. And when seasoned with prayer, your actions yield astonishing results!**

Since, then, you have been raised with Christ, set your hearts on things above, where Christ is seated at the right hand of God. Set your minds on things above, not on earthly things. For you died, and your life is now hidden with Christ in God. When Christ, who is your life, appears, then you also will appear with him in glory.

-COLOSSIANS 3:1-4, NIV

Think eternally *now*. Be heavenly minded in all you do. You will remain balanced if you keep closely connected with other believers in a good, solid Bible-teaching church. The Lord and your neighbor need you, daily filled with and obedient to the Spirit.

What is God asking you to do today? What is He saying about this message? To whom can you minister life?

1. Lewis, *Mere Christianity*, 134.

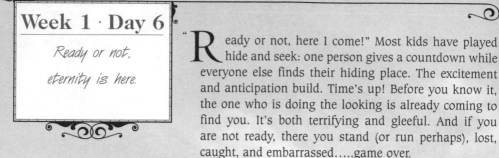

## Week 1 · Day 6

*Ready or not,
eternity is here.*

"Ready or not, here I come!" Most kids have played hide and seek: one person gives a countdown while everyone else finds their hiding place. The excitement and anticipation build. Time's up! Before you know it, the one who is doing the looking is already coming to find you. It's both terrifying and gleeful. And if you are not ready, there you stand (or run perhaps), lost, caught, and embarrassed......game over.

That childhood game is good preparation for life. We live daily with looming deadlines. It is reality, like having to eat and sleep. No one can escape the everyday movement of time and its obligations and demands.

Most spend a lifetime simply meeting their daily obligations, so involved in the immediate that no thought is given for the bigger picture. But that is flirting with disaster, because eternity is here now, regardless of what anyone believes. From the moment you were conceived, then drew breath and became aware, the game was on. For believers, here is a great word:

> And all who believe in God's Son have eternal life. Those who don't obey the Son will never experience eternal life but the wrath of God remains upon them
>
> -John 3:36, NLT

What would it be like to suddenly stand at the throne of God? There you will no longer be able to run or hide but will be caught "ready or not". From there, your eternal destiny is secure.

Christians believe that everyone is destined for eternal endless existence. For those who are in Christ it is truly eternal life and bliss. For those who reject Christ it is also endless – eternal misery – the unspeakable horror of separation from God and God's people forever and ever. The lost are the hopeless living-dead, unchangeable, with no appeal available.

**Once you die, your eternal fate is fixed. What is your condition?**

## Week 1 · Day 7

*Don't just read for a mental understanding, which can be easily forgotten or lost, but let His Word be hidden in your heart through contemplation and prayer.*

-JOHN BEVERE

There are a lot of things in circulation about heaven, hell, eternal life, and related subjects. Ecclesiastes has an interesting word relating to this. The twelfth chapter, twelfth verse says in part, *"Of making many books there is no end, and much study is wearisome to the flesh."*

We do have a biblical mandate to do our homework. Regardless of the complexity or sheer volume of the subject, we are required to seek and find wisdom.

> Be diligent to present yourself approved to God, a worker who does not need to be ashamed, rightly dividing the word of truth.
> -2 TIMOTHY 2:15

Is some effort required? Sure, but this is great news for us all. The Bible is our pre-eminent source, and its truths are attainable to each of us. The issues that are subjects of great controversy and that seem so difficult could be rendered much more simply, practically, and useful if we first look to the Word of God.

> This "foolish" plan of God is far wiser than the wisest of human plans, and God's weakness is far stronger than the greatest of human strength. Remember, dear brothers and sisters, that few of you were wise in the world's eyes, or powerful, or wealthy when God called you. Instead, God deliberately chose things the world considers foolish in order to shame those who think they are wise. And he chose those who are powerless to shame those who are powerful.
> -1 CORINTHIANS 1:25-27, NLT

*Driven by Eternity:*
## YOUR WEEK IN REVIEW

- There is a time of God's favor, and when it is at hand we must respond to it. Contemplation, prayer, and godly action are how we respond.

- Time will pass, and everyone will eventually face death. But God has graciously given us time to prepare for both death and the eternal destiny that comes at death.

- At times life isn't easy. There are many trials to live through and decisions to make. But following Christ can be as straightforward as the child's game of "follow the leader." Follow Jesus daily, and you will naturally end up where He is. Our choices in the "now" – our daily life – determine our eternal destiny.

- Living a biblical lifestyle impacts the world.

- Keep your heart and mind on things eternal. When God moves through you it is meaningful. You will make a difference in others' eternal destinies!

- Whether you are ready or not, eternity does not wait for us.

The topics we are contemplating may be challenging. Let God's Word take deep root in your heart by prayer and study and meditating daily on these truths.

Take a look at your journaling from the last six days. Summarize here what God is saying to you this week. You will find it so valuable if you make the effort to think and pray it through so you can put it in a few powerful sentences.

_____

_____

_____

_____

_____

If there are any specific directions or actions the Lord is leading you to take, record those as well. Be sure to follow through on them. Perhaps tell a friend or prayer partner who can pray with you and for you and help you keep your commitments.

_____

_____

_____

_____

## THE WEEK IN PRAYER

*Father, in Jesus' name I ask You to keep me focused on eternal things. I need Your Spirit's empowerment, I desire Your presence. Help me to rightly divide the Word of Truth and make the right choices in life. I look to You for direction in all things, and I submit to Your will. I forsake worldly ways of thinking and ask for Your thoughts, which are higher than mine. I sow Your Word deeply in the soil of my heart, and I trust You to make me as a tree planted by the living waters. By Your grace I want to bring forth much fruit in due season and to prosper.*

*I want to live a life that counts, today and forever. I ask, Lord, to be a believer who is driven by eternity. Amen.*

*Teach us to make the most of our time, so that we may grow in wisdom.*
*-PSALM 90:12, NLT*

## Making the Most of Our Time

In the afternoon I preached to the Indians...afterward...the power of God seemed to descend upon the assembly "like a rushing mighty wind," and with an astonishing energy bore down all before it. I stood amazed at the influence which seized the audience almost universally; and could compare it to nothing more aptly than the irresistible force of a mighty torrent, or swelling deluge...Almost all persons of all ages were bowed down with concern together, and scarcely one was able to withstand the shock of this surprising operation. Old men and women who had been drunken wretches for many years, and some little children...appeared in distress for their souls, as well as persons of middle age.

The most stubborn hearts were now obliged to bow. A principal man among the Indians...who with great confidence the day before told me "he had been a Christian more than ten years;" was now brought under solemn concern for his soul, and wept bitterly. Another...who had been a murderer, conjurer and a notorious drunkard was likewise brought now to cry for mercy with many tears...when he saw his danger so very great.

They were almost all universally crying and praying for mercy in every part of the house, and many out of doors; and numbers could neither go nor stand.
-AUGUST 8, 1745, FROM THE DIARY OF DAVID BRAINERD

I have now rode more than three thousand miles, of which I have kept an exact account, since the beginning of March last, and almost the whole of it has been in my own proper business as a missionary, upon the design...of propagating *Christian knowledge* among the Indians.
-NOVEMBER 4, 1745, FROM THE DIARY OF DAVID BRAINERD

Some people have taken the promises of God and used them more for living for the day instead of looking at it through an eternal scope.
-JOHN BEVERE

**David Brainerd: A Man With Eternal Perspective, Little Time, and Major Impact!**

It is said that when John Wesley, the great world-changer and founder of the Methodist

Church, wanted to keep the fires of revival burning, he told preachers to carefully read the diary of David Brainerd. Few men or women have used their short time on earth to the glory of God as well as Brainerd, born in 1718, did. At only twenty-nine years of age, this man – to whom no less than genius Jonathan Edwards gave the highest of recommendations – died of illness, having left a mark on history more meaningful than most who live two or three times his age.

## A true counterculture lifestyle

Though brilliant and well connected, Brainerd chose to forsake worldly ambition and comforts and instead follow God. His exceedingly difficult wilderness ministry to the American Indians was almost daily marked with savage conditions and threats to life. Hostile places and at times hostile people, hunger, cold, primitive or no shelter, few maps, despite all this and more – language barriers, arduous travel on foot and horse-back, poverty, and social and cultural obstacles – his short life's work was nonetheless blessed by God and is venerated even today, hundreds of years later in modern society. Countless people, including many prominent ministers, have been deeply influenced by his short life.

> *All that is outside of Him is temporal and will change. No matter how good, noble, powerful, or enduring it may seem, it will eventually cease.*
>
> —JOHN BEVERE

1.  What do you think about David Brainerd's lifestyle?

2.  In only a few short years David Brainerd impacted those around him and then the world in deeply meaningful ways that continue to have eternal significance. When you consider the amazing things he endured and the wonderful ways God blessed him, does it discourage or encourage you? Why?

Learning from good examples and finding motivation are some of the irreplaceable benefits to beholding the great cloud of witnesses that God has sent before us. But remember, we are not competing or comparing ourselves with others. It is you alone who will answer to God one day. God has plans and purposes for your life, right where you are, right now.

Have fun with the following question. Let your God-inspired imagination freely envision how God could flow through you to make eternal impact on the world. Be "realistic" only in the sense of not being overtly foolish, but also be bold and think outside the box. You never know exactly what good things God has for your future, and this could really open up your heart and mind to new opportunities.

3.  We are not all called to live as missionaries, but do you dream of having extraordinary God-adventures? What do they look like? Write them down here; then share them and discuss them with others.

    _____

    _____

    _____

Brainerd faced seemingly impossible odds, yet he was filled with purpose and driven by eternal values. We may never be faced with hardships like his. Yet we find all kinds of reasons – excuses – why we can't serve God.

4.  Are you living with an eternal perspective?

    _____

    _____

    _____

5.  What is encouraging or preventing you from making the most of your time and living a life that counts?

    _____

    _____

    _____

6.  Now here's an exciting challenge for you. Do your best to describe YOUR life's calling in detail. What is it you believe you are ultimately supposed to be doing in life? What is encouraging you or preventing you from making the most of your time and living a life that counts?

    _____

    _____

    _____

> Day by day the Lord observes the good deeds done by godly men, and gives them eternal rewards.
>
> -PSALM 37:18, TLB

7.  What can you learn and, more importantly, apply from the lives of people like David Brainerd?

    _____

    _____

    _____

    _____

> If anyone hears me and doesn't obey me, I am not his judge – for I have come to save the world and not to judge it. But all who reject me and my message will be judged at the day of judgment by the truth I have spoken.
>
> -JOHN 12:47-48, NLT

8.  According to John 12:47-48, what God has already spoken in His Word will be the criteria for our judgment. How does this make you feel knowing the judgments given on this day will be forever?

    _____

    _____

    _____

9.  Many people – often without really realizing it – believe pastors, and missionaries in particular, have a "corner on the market," that they are the ones who are truly spiritual, living right, and making the most of their time on this earth. How much truth do you think there is in that, and why?

    _____

    _____

    _____

---

**hot TOPIC** Some believers may be more surprised at the judgment than unbelievers. Why? How could this be?

_____

_____

_____

_____

---

**ZENITH**
the time when
something is
most powerful
or successful.

What in this first hour was most powerful to you? How is it meaningful to your eternal success?

_____

_____

_____

_____

_____

_____

_____

# LIFE IN ENDEL

A wondrous enchanted land of incomparable

beauty, peace, prosperity, and the presence

of the great King — it sounds so desirable!

Let's enter this kingdom and see what

we find within its borders...and

within our own hearts and lives.

PLEASE REFER TO CHAPTER 2 IN THE
*Driven by Eternity* BOOK OR THE *Affabel* CD SET

# You and the Five Students

Some readers will see themselves almost totally in the lives of one of the five students of Endel. Others will see portions of some or even all of them in their own lives and hearts.

God longs to open our eyes to our true motives so He can bless us and change us more into His glorious image. Observe closely the descriptions of the students. **Let the characterization of the students act as a powerful and revealing light being shown upon your own heart.**

1. Write in the spaces below any ways you are similar to the students in both the good or not-so-good traits. Record what the Lord speaks to you about this message. *God is providing you with a priceless opportunity to prepare in advance and correct your course now for the day you go to meet Him in judgment!*

   • Independent


   • Deceived


   • Faint Heart


   • Selfish


   • Charity

Now what is the Holy Spirit saying to you about what you've seen? Are there ways you are being led to change, submitting to the Word and Spirit and being empowered by God's grace? Take some time to record all God is saying to you.

# Swept Toward the Final Day

2  As you read the parable, how do you feel as the Royal Guard gathers the two thousand students, takes them to Affabel, and then divides them into two groups in two different halls?

3  What do you think God is trying to say to you as you read this part of the story?

4 Some in the Hall of Justice thought that anything that was confusing or seemed out of step could be attributed to Jalyn's mercy or the mystery of His ways. This reasoning comforted them, but do you think it will hold up?

5 Why?

**Time of prayer:** "Lord God, I come to You totally open to the Holy Spirit. I ask You to reveal what is truly within me and help me see myself and my life as You do. Reveal, Lord, the things You want me to see from the lives of the five students in this story. I can take it, Lord. I am ready by Your grace. Show me the things You want me to see, the things You want me to face. And help me to write it down and to then be changed by Your Holy Spirit and Your Word so I can be more like You, and spend eternity with You. I ask You to send out Your light and truth and let them lead me, Lord. In Jesus' name I pray, amen."

Please refer to page 279 for info on ordering your *Affabel* CD Set

# THE DAY OF JUDGMENT 1

The great King Jalyn and 100,000 citizens

of the incredible city of Affabel;

what will happen in the Great Hall,

and what does it mean to YOU?

---

PLEASE REFER TO CHAPTER 3 IN THE
*Driven by Eternity* BOOK OR THE *Affabel* CD SET

# INDEPENDENT MEETS THE GREAT KING

Independent had heard of the King and of the great city Affabel; he had even been taught about them. But he had busily gone his own way in life, figuring everything would turn out all right in the end. However, when he saw Affabel was a real place and beheld the majesty of the city, its people, and the great King, he was forced to believe it all. Now at the end of his time, Independent is brought before the King, and suddenly it is demanded that he give an account of his time in Endel.

So he called him and said to him, "What is this I hear about you? Give an account of your stewardship, for you can no longer be steward."

-LUKE 16:2

Every detail of his life is exposed. He is horrified at his behavior even though he sees some good deeds as well. *But his name is not found in the Book of Life.*

Clinging to his few good works, Independent musters the courage to respond to Jalyn.

*1* What happens at every point he brings up?

Independent finally concedes – Jalyn is right. Then he remembers something he had heard one of his few times he went to class: Jalyn is merciful! Perhaps He'd scold and punish Independent, then surely show His mercy!

*2* Why doesn't this happen the way Independent imagined?

Jalyn patiently explains how Independent was incorrect about true mercy and justice.

*3* Why is it justice and mercy when God judges that an unbeliever should go to hell? Why can't God "just let them in" to heaven?

Many people live every day with Independent's same self-willed lifestyle. They have false ideas about the kingdom of God, the mercy of Jesus, and what justice really means. Independent wasn't a "bad" person. Nor did he do "terrible" things. He even did some good things and was a respected member of the community! But none of those things are the point. His life clearly showed that ultimately he had chosen an evil nature, believing his own counsel and going his own way, not the way of the King.

Job 21:13-15 (NIV) says "They spend their years in prosperity and go down to the grave in peace. Yet they say to God, 'Leave us alone! We have no desire to know your ways. Who is the Almighty, that we should serve him? What would we gain by praying to him?'"

4  What was Independent's fatal mistake in life?

5  What are your feelings as Independent is struck with terror and horror, realizing his fate when he is bound hand and foot and taken away?

# DECEIVED BEFORE JALYN

Independent had thought that because Jalyn was merciful He would overlook Independent's sin. Deceived thought he would find favor with Jalyn because he professed belief in Him.

6  What was Deceived guilty of?

7  Jalyn asked Deceived why he called Him Lord. What was the point of this question, and what can you learn from it for your life, right now?

8  Remember Ruthless, whom Deceived met on his way into the hall and whose name was changed to Reconciled? How did his short time serving Jalyn differ from Deceived's whole life?

9  Deceived's every objection – even when he boldly quoted Jalyn's own words – is countered with quotations from the law of God. Could it be possible that we can believe in God and not be saved, just as Deceived did?

If so, how can that happen?

10 How does this verse, "You believe that there is one God. You do well. Even the demons believe – and tremble!" (James 2:19), apply to Deceived?

Look at James chapter 2 in the Amplified Bible.

So also faith, if it does not have works (deeds and actions of obedience to back it up), by itself is destitute of power (inoperative, dead). But someone will say [to you then], You [say you] have faith, and I have [good] works. Now you show me your [alleged] faith apart from any [good] works [if you can], and I by [good] works [of obedience] will show you my faith.
Are you willing to be shown [proof], you foolish (unproductive, spiritually deficient) fellow, that faith apart from [good] works is inactive and ineffective and worthless? Thus also faith by itself, if it does not have works, is dead.
-JAMES 2:17-18, 20

Our lifestyle will accuse us or vindicate us. It shows either the proof of our faith or the proof that we simply claimed faith but lived a life that denied the Lord. But to the wicked God says:

"What right have you to declare My statutes,
Or take My covenant in your mouth,
Seeing you hate instruction
And cast My words behind you?
When you saw a thief, you consented with him,
And have been a partaker with adulterers.
You give your mouth to evil,
And your tongue frames deceit.
You sit and speak against your brother;
You slander your own mother's son.
These things you have done, and I kept silent;
You thought that I was altogether like you;
But I will rebuke you,
And set them in order before your eyes.
Now consider this, you who forget God,
Lest I tear you in pieces,
And there be none to deliver:
Whoever offers praise glorifies Me;
And to him who orders his conduct aright
I will show the salvation of God."

-PSALM 50:16-23

**11** **We don't have to be deceived.** *Take this time to examine your heart.* As you are going through each part of this book, God is giving you the opportunity to not neglect your salvation. **What is the Lord showing you about your own heart, your own lifestyle?**

# Faint Heart's Judgment

However, if righteous people turn to sinful ways and start acting like other sinners, should they be allowed to live? No, of course not! All their previous goodness will be forgotten, and they will die for their sins. Yet you say, "The Lord isn't being just!" Listen to me, O people of Israel. Am I the one who is unjust, or is it you? When righteous people turn from being good and start doing sinful things, they will die for it. Yes, they will die because of their sinful deeds. And if wicked people turn away from their wickedness, obey the law, and do what is just and right, they will save their lives.

-EZEKIEL 18:24-27, NLT

**12** What was Faint Heart's fatal mistake?

Dear friends, if we deliberately continue sinning after we have received a full knowledge of the truth, there is no other sacrifice that will cover these sins. There will be nothing to look forward to but the terrible expectation of God's judgment and the raging fire that will consume his enemies. Anyone who refused to obey the law of Moses was put to death without mercy on the testimony of two or three witnesses. Think how much more terrible the punishment will be for those who have trampled on the Son of God and have treated the blood of the covenant as if it were common and unholy. Such people have insulted and enraged the Holy Spirit who brings God's mercy to his people.

For we know the one who said, "I will take vengeance. I will repay those who deserve it."

He also said, "The Lord will judge his own people."

It is a terrible thing to fall into the hands of the living God.

-HEBREWS 10:26-31, NLT

Take some time to reflect, as there is nothing more important than eternal destiny. Journal your thoughts, questions, concerns, and prayers and let God minister to your need as you consider this:

*Though no one can take you out of God's hand, still, you can walk away.* Faint Heart chose to exalt her bitterness and unforgiveness above Jalyn's teachings. She chose to lived offended and in rebellion to Jalyn, when all she needed to do was ask for Jalyn's help and repent.

God has given you the awesome power of a free will. There are many things into which we may stumble and fall, but we can call on the name of the Lord for help and continue to love Him and follow His ways. Examine your own life.

13   Like Faint Heart, could your name be erased from the Book of Life? Why or why not?

# Double Life's Condemnation

14   While Faint Heart gave up her salvation, Double Life is quite another story. One of the most gifted teachers in Endel, Double Life seemed well prepared for judgment day. But what went wrong?

15   Why?

16   Which did Double Life love more, Jalyn or the position Jalyn had given him? What are some of the things you can see in his life that show Double Life loved the power, influence, and other benefits of his position at the school of Endel, yet also show his motives were wrong and that he took the teachings, grace, and mercy of Jalyn for granted?

Double Life reminds us of Judas Iscariot. Ultimately Judas didn't love Jesus; he loved what he could get from Jesus. Though chosen by Jesus and privileged to work closely with Him for three and a half years, Judas truly lived a *double life*. Look at just a few verses:

> Then He called His twelve disciples together and gave them power and authority over all demons, and to cure diseases.
>
> -LUKE 9:1

> But one of His disciples, Judas Iscariot, Simon's son, who would betray Him, said, "Why was this fragrant oil not sold for three hundred denarii and given to the poor?" This he said, not that he cared for the poor, but because he was a thief, and had the money box; and he used to take what was put in it.
>
> -JOHN 12:4-6

> Then one of the twelve, called Judas Iscariot, went to the chief priests and said, "What are you willing to give me if I deliver Him to you?" And they counted out to him thirty pieces of silver. So from that time he sought opportunity to betray Him.
>
> -MATTHEW 26:14-16

At the very same time Judas was praising the Lord, preaching the gospel, healing the sick, casting out devils, and working closely with Jesus, he was stealing from Jesus and was a deceitful, treacherous flatterer. Like Double Life, everyone thought Judas a great disciple and follower of their Master, yet their King knew better.

Matthew 26:24 declares, "It would have been good for that man if he had not been born." Matthew 23:14 speaks to the religious leaders who serve God out of the motive of gain and take advantage of people in the name of the Lord: "Therefore you will receive greater condemnation." These men and women, just like Double Life, will find themselves in the darkest and most tormenting places of hell.

The Scriptures speak plainly about how each of us must live a consecrated, disciplined, and repentant life in Christ. A lifestyle of sin is still a lifestyle of sin, even if – and especially if – you are a great teacher of God's Word.

> "You must be ready all the time, for the Son of Man will come when least expected."
>
> Peter asked, "Lord, is this illustration just for us or for everyone?"
>
> And the Lord replied, "I'm talking to any faithful, sensible servant to whom the master gives the responsibility of managing his household and feeding his family. If the master returns and finds that the servant has done a good job, there will be a reward. I assure you, the master will put that servant in charge of all he owns. But if the servant thinks, 'My master won't be back for a while,' and begins oppressing the other servants, partying, and getting drunk – well, the master will return unannounced and unexpected. He will tear the servant apart and banish him with the unfaithful. The servant will be severely punished, for though he knew his duty, he refused to do it.
>
> "But people who are not aware that they are doing wrong will be punished only lightly. Much is required from those to whom much is given, and much more is required from those to whom much more is given."
>
> -LUKE 12:40-48, NLT

17  How does Luke 12:40-48 apply to Double Life?

## $\mathcal{W}$HAT $\mathcal{A}$BOUT $\mathcal{Y}$OU

The self-deception, blindness, and self-justification in all of the people in these judgments only led to a horrible end.

When he arrives at Lone, Independent is told the terrible place is exactly as he had been forewarned in Endel. **How has God forewarned you through this message?** Have these stories and Scriptures you've encountered in *Driven by Eternity* opened your eyes to new things?

18  What are some of the specific things you are seeing as they apply to your life?

19  How are you handling it?

20  Consider what you are going to do about what you've now learned, and take action. Remember, eternity is at stake.

### Prayer

Father God, I thank You for showing me these sobering truths from Your Word. I thank You for intervening in my life at this moment. Your great mercy shows me the path of life. Your goodness shows me how to flee from the path of destruction. I know I have choices to make, Lord, and I pray right now for the empowerment of Your grace to make the right choices and to keep them by Your Spirit's strength. Help me to live according to Your Word and in the power of the Holy Spirit. Reveal to me the things You want me to learn and to do as I go through this teaching.

Lord, I give my life to You wholeheartedly. I will forsake my ways for Your ways. I trust that You who began a good work in me will complete it so I will one day stand before You and be blessed, not cursed. Thank You, Lord. In Jesus' name, amen.

Please refer to page 279 for info on ordering your *Affabel* CD Set

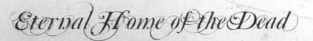

*Eternal Home of the Dead*

# HOUR 2

Please refer to Chapter 4,

Eternal Home of the Dead,

in the *Driven by Eternity* book

and video session 2.

## Week 2 · Day 1

*Many — and I am including devoted followers of Christ — are unaware of these issues.*

-JOHN BEVERE

Even in today's extremely information-driven society we can be unaware of innumerable important events. Entire countries may have revolutions, thousands die of starvation, rulers come and go. Our own town can pass resolutions affecting our very home, and it escapes us until the reality of it is thrust upon us in the form of a citation or legal notice. Not only does this apply to events, but it also often applies to critical knowledge we could greatly benefit from. Who can keep up with the worlds of art, health, finance, and countless other areas? The sheer volume of data in our "Information Age" world is overwhelming indeed and barely comprehendible.

It is imperative we choose wisely what we are going to give our minds, hearts, and lives to. We can only take in so much. People tend to fall into one of three categories. Running ragged trying to discern when, where, how, and what we will take into our lives and follow, or shutting down and retreating from life, or some rather delicate balance between the two. Each of these leads to frustration and discontent. But for the devoted follower of Christ, there is good news.

> If then you were raised with Christ, seek those things which are above, where Christ is, sitting at the right hand of God. Set your mind on things above, not on things on the earth. For you died, and your life is hidden with Christ in God. When Christ who is our life appears, then you also will appear with Him in glory.
>
> -COLOSSIANS 3:1-4

The Word of God is our ready-made "filter" through which we can pass all of life's choices. The disciple of Christ knows what is most important to seek and find. God's priorities have become ours. While it is certain we cannot keep up with all of the world's flow of information, it is also true we know where our priorities lie and where our energies must be devoted: to the things of God, heavenly things, biblical things. On our subject of eternity, heaven, and hell, there is no reason we should remain ignorant of the foundational truths of God's Word.

If you miss a piece of financial information, it could cost you a few thousand dollars. If you miss a piece of health information, it could cost you a few years of life. **Of all the information clamoring for your attention, if you do not pay heed to the call of God's Word, it could cost you your very body, soul, and rewards for eternity!**

What are you giving your attentions to? What is the Holy Spirit desiring to say about it?

_____

_____

_____

_____

_____

## Week 2 · Day 2

*Eternity will not be long enough for us to ever stop regretting it if on this earth we have wasted time.'*

-FRANCOIS FENELON

In our last devotion the apostle Paul told us in Collossians 3:1-4 we have died to our old life and been raised with Christ, and our new life is now hidden with Christ in God. Not only does he give those facts, but he also emphatically declares the response they demand from us. We are to seek and set our minds on things that are eternal.

Paul's language speaks of our attitude toward how we spend our energies in life. We are either eternally minded or not; it's as simple as that. To live a life or even a day driven by anything other than eternity is dangerous indeed – terrifying even – if you consider heaven and hell.

The very next verses of Scripture continue the message:

> Put to death, therefore, whatever belongs to your earthly nature: sexual immorality, impurity, lust, evil desires and greed, which is idolatry. Because of these, the wrath of God is coming. You used to walk in these ways, in the life you once lived. But now you must rid yourselves of all such things as these: anger, rage, malice, slander, and filthy language from your lips. Do not lie to each other, since you have taken off your old self with its practices and have put on the new self, which is being renewed in knowledge in the image of its Creator.
>
> -COLOSSIANS 3:5-10, NIV

Notice it does not say that God does everything for us. Rather, God has given us a part to play in daily life. Far from being robotic creatures that are enslaved to God's will, instead we are given choices in our daily lifestyle by God. **God desires a people who desire Him. If we are in Christ, we are to seek God's heart and God's ways, the things of eternal significance.** The power to do this comes from God's grace.

Our daily life plainly reveals where our mind is set and what we are seeking in life. One day, for certain, all will be judged by God Himself. He has already told us that the Scriptures He has given are the standard by which we will be held accountable. His judgments will be forever unalterable: wrath or blessing, heaven or hell, unceasing misery apart from God or glory with Christ forever. By God's grace, we have a choice to make daily.

For sure God isn't looking for perfect people. He is looking for hearts that are strong toward Him and a people who are willing to be obedient to His Word. He empowers us to overcome by His grace. We can grow in the things of the Lord. Think of Jesus quietly following you around, observing your daily life. Would it plainly reveal a person who is seeking the things of God and whose mind is set on eternity? What would He see? What do you think He would say? How could He help you? Be open to His Word; pray and seek Him now.

1. Francois Fenelon, *Meditations on the Heart of God*, Christian Classics (Orleans, MA: Paraclete Press, 1997), chapter 36, "Time Is Precious."

## Week 2 · Day 3

*Most believers are not fully aware of eternal judgments and rewards. [The apostle] Paul said these are things you should have been aware of a long time ago.*

-JOHN BEVERE

It's easy to believe that because you've sat in church or read the Bible for years you are "all set." Beware of such a perilous deception! Think of Jesus and the "spiritual" leaders of His day. There is a vast difference between being "religious" and being a disciple of Jesus Christ. The religious person takes on many forms and can end up self-deceived and on the wrong road. The scribes and Pharisees were extremely well versed in Scripture and very dutiful in the Law. They were respected by many and were sure they were "somebody" in God's kingdom. But Jesus said they were lost and were "like whitewashed tombs, which look beautiful on the outside but on the inside are full of dead men's bones and everything unclean" (Matt. 23:27, NIV).

The true disciple is markedly different, ever humble in the fear of God and ever seeking loving fellowship with God and God's people. The disciple desires God's truth and relies on God's empowering grace to live a passionate life that loves what God loves and hates what God hates. A disciple's life will look like his Master's.

Today it is very possible to be steeped in your church's teaching but not know the basics of the faith. Some foundational truths may have been under emphasized or even omitted. One example is the subject of eternal judgment. Many new and seasoned believers have never understood that eternity – eternal judgment – is one of the elementary school lessons of the Bible.

> So let us stop going over the basics of Christianity again and again. Let us go on instead and become mature in our understanding. Surely we don't need to start all over again with the importance of turning away from evil deeds and placing our faith in God. You don't need further instruction about baptisms, the laying on of hands, the resurrection of the dead, and eternal judgment. And so, God willing, we will move forward to further understanding.
>
> -HEBREWS 6:1-3, NLT

> And as it is appointed unto men once to die, but after this the judgment.
> -HEBREWS 9:27, KJV

> Because he hath appointed a day, in the which he will judge the world in righteousness by that man whom he hath ordained; whereof he hath given assurance unto all men, in that he hath raised him from the dead.
> -ACTS 17:31, KJV

The InterVarsity Press New Testament Commentary on Acts 17:31 puts it this way: "The call to repentance is urgent because the consequences for not repenting – a final judgment and eternal condemnation – are inescapable. The judgment is definite (*he has set a day*; Lk 17:24, 30; 21:34-36), universal (*he will judge the world*, or "whole inhabited world"; Acts

11:28; 17:6), fair (*with justice*; Ps 96:13) and personal (*by the man he has appointed*, Jesus; Jn 5:27; Acts 10:42)."[1]

**There are many things you can let slide, many things you can put off until later. But the subject – the truth – of eternal judgment is not one of them.** *Search the Scriptures, and let them search your heart.* These few moments in the Bible can bring you endless moments in glorious eternity. Ask God to open the eyes of your heart. Write your contemplations:

1. William J. Larkin Jr., *Acts*, IVP New Testament Commentary Series (Downers Grove, IL: InterVarsity Press, 1995), 260, s.v. "Acts 17:16-34."

## Week 2 · Day 4

*Hell is a real place; it's not figurative.*

-JOHN BEVERE

Contemporary society's attitude toward heaven and hell could be called complacent at best. Few truly believe in them as literal places, and many scoff. Most have vague ideas or concepts about them and generally treat them as something not really important to daily life. There is a massive need for clear instruction and powerful biblical answers to questions – both modern and ancient – people have on the subject. Nearly two thousand years ago the sophisticates of Athens were much the same as many in today's society. The apostle Paul masterfully engaged them in this life-or-death subject.

In Acts 17 he brilliantly yet simply told his "modern" audience of thinkers, skeptics, and religious people about Christ's teachings. It may offend people's sensibilities when we talk about heaven and hell – eternal glory versus endless torment – yet when Paul preached, some believed and were saved.

When it comes to the subject of hell in particular, no group has cornered the market of denial or ignorance. Its existence is held in derision by celebrated and brilliant thinkers, the rich and famous, the uneducated, and the poor and downtrodden alike. **Yet the most influential person who ever lived plainly spoke often of hell as a very real place.** Hear the words of Jesus:

> Do not be afraid of those who kill the body but cannot kill the soul. Rather, be afraid of the One who can destroy both soul and body in hell.
>
> -MATTHEW 10:28, NIV

> You snakes! You brood of vipers! How will you escape being condemned to hell?
>
> -MATTHEW 23:33, NIV

> And if your eye causes you to sin, pluck it out. It is better for you to enter the kingdom of God with one eye than to have two eyes and be thrown into hell, where "their worm does not die, and the fire is not quenched."
>
> -MARK 9:47-48, NIV

> Then he will say to those on his left, "Depart from me, you who are cursed, into the eternal fire prepared for the devil and his angels"…Then they will go away to eternal punishment, but the righteous to eternal life.
>
> -MATTHEW 25:41, 46, NIV

> In hell, where he was in torment, he looked up and saw Abraham far away, with Lazarus by his side. So he called to him, "Father Abraham, have pity on me and send Lazarus to dip the tip of his finger in water and cool my tongue, because I am in agony in this fire."
>
> -LUKE 16:23-24, NIV

There are people who live in countries of wealth, beauty, and freedom. In other places, distant, almost unreal, many are born into untold suffering in impoverished, diseased, and war-torn lands. **Just because you don't see distant lands, just because they seem hard to believe, doesn't mean they aren't real places with real people in real agony right now. You can't choose where you will be born. But you can choose the land in which you will spend eternity.**

*"Misery loves company" is not true in hell.*

-JOHN BEVERE

H ow do you do a day's devotional about eternal hell? The subjects of horror movies, nights of the living dead, and the dawn of the forever damned hardly seem like the stuff of quiet time with the Lord!

Yet Jesus spoke openly and gravely about it. *Gravely* means "requiring serious thought, something momentous, fraught with danger." **Death and the grave are something we ALL will face.** And that is exactly how Jesus presented the subject of hell. He wanted people to know and seriously consider their imminent peril. And Jesus wanted people to decide whether to follow Him – ultimately to heaven – or not.

Paul spoke about this, too. In fact, this most important book ever written, the book that is always on the best-seller list and has changed the lives of untold millions, is full of the topic, from beginning to end.

In the beginning, in Genesis, the serpent enters the garden and man falls from grace. Sixty-six books later, Revelation 20:10 says:

> The devil, who deceived them, was cast into the lake of fire and brimstone where the beast and the false prophet are. And they will be tormented day and night forever and ever.

From start to finish the Bible shows us God's overriding concern for our destiny. Yes, man fell. Yes, there are consequences for our sin. But God has provided Himself as the answer to our "problem."

> This is good and pleases God our Savior, for he wants everyone to be saved and to understand the truth. For there is only one God and one Mediator who can reconcile God and people. He is the man Christ Jesus. He gave his life to purchase freedom for everyone. This is the message that God gave to the world at the proper time.
>
> -1 TIMOTHY 2:3-6, NLT

Urban myths and legends may amuse us. Foolish tales can waste our time. It has been said Jesus was either a madman who claimed to be God Himself or He was who He said He was. There is really no in-between. And if He is who He claimed, then He holds the keys to heaven and hell, and we'd best take heed to His words.

> I am he that liveth, and was dead; and, behold, I am alive for evermore, Amen; and have the keys of hell and of death.
>
> -REVELATION 1:18, KJV

Who better to comfort us in our problems or miseries than our loved ones? Not so in hell. In Luke 16:28 the man in agony in hell (Hades) begged that his brothers be warned so they would not join him. Hell is the land of the alone, where alone one must face eternity's endless terrors. Jesus made plain His desire for us to face these things. Take some time and do it now. **Today is the day for obedience to Jesus in all things.** How is He leading you at this moment?

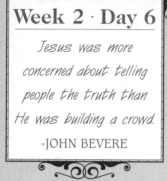

## Week 2 · Day 6

*Jesus was more concerned about telling people the truth than He was building a crowd.*

-JOHN BEVERE

The truth is best for us. It may be painful, but how joyful we are when things turn out right because of it. Jesus never sugarcoated the simple truth. It is one of the reasons many attempts were made to take his life (Matt. 12:14; Luke 4:28-30; John 5:18; 7; 8:37, 40; 11:47-53). His truths often upset the status quo. Regardless of consequences, Jesus was a man of truth. And not only did He speak it, but He also lived it. Born of a virgin, God as His Father, Jesus Christ was 100 percent God, 100 percent man. After He was crucified, dead for three days, and entombed, hundreds of people witnessed to the fact that He lived again, raised from the dead.

God, Jesus, mankind, heaven, hell, truth, salvation? How is it all possible?

> But Jesus looked at them and said to them, "With men this is impossible, but with God all things are possible."
>
> -MATTHEW 19:26

His disciples asked Jesus about salvation. It all seemed amazing and too difficult. But Jesus said, "With God all things are possible." Perhaps the key here is in the *"with* God" portion of that verse. It is possible to live a life calling yourself (and having others call you) a Christian, but not really living *with* the Lord. "With" means next to, alongside of, having as a possession the same details or characteristics.

*Matthew Henry's Concise Commentary* says this about Matthew 19: "It is required of us in following Christ, that we duly attend his ordinances, strictly follow his pattern, and cheerfully submit to his disposals; and this from love to him, and in dependence on him."[1]

That is very different than what we mostly hear today. Jesus asked in Luke 6:46 why anyone would call Him Lord yet not do the things He says. Look at another verse:

> "Many will say to Me in that day, 'Lord, Lord, have we not prophesied in Your name, cast out demons in Your name, and done many wonders in Your name?' And then I will declare to them, 'I never knew you; depart from Me, you who practice lawlessness!'
>
> "Therefore whoever hears these sayings of Mine, and does them, I will liken him to a wise man who built his house on the rock: and the rain descended, the floods came, and the winds blew and beat on that house; and it did not fall, for it was founded on the rock.
>
> "But everyone who hears these sayings of Mine, and does not do them, will be like a foolish man who built his house on the sand: and the rain descended, the floods came, and the winds blew and beat on that house; and it fell. And great was its fall."
>
> And so it was, when Jesus had ended these sayings, that the people were astonished at His teaching.
>
> -MATTHEW 7:22-28

**To make heaven, not hell, it isn't enough to be astonished at His teachings. You**

**must also *follow* them!** Are there specific commandments you know you need God's strength to live out?

---

1. Matthew Henry, *Matthew Henry's Concise Commentary on the Whole Bible* (Nashville, TN: Nelson Reference, 2000).

# Week 2 · Day 7

*Jalyn responded, "I am a merciful king, and that is exactly why I'm sending you away. By choosing to spend your time in Endel the way you did, you permanently chose your nature, that of the dark lord Dagon. How could I be merciful, true, and loving if I allowed your immoral fiber to pollute the purity of this great city? I would put the innocent of Affabel in harm's way. Your chosen nature would soon manifest and thus corrupt thousands of pure lives. You have chosen your own way. You will be recompensed for it exactly as the one you followed, Dagon. If I give you less than I gave him, then I would be an unjust leader, and that I am not!"*

-THE JUDGMENT OF
INDEPENDENT

Who would question the justice given out by any judge with irrefutable evidence of an offender's guilt? Though we may cringe at the awfulness and finality of the sentence for the convicted, we readily acknowledge the demand for justice. A double standard will never work. If justice is anything it must be consistent, with the same measure for all.

Life is filled with choices for which God will hold us accountable. Romans 3:23 tells us that all have fallen short of the glory of God. And so Christ came for us all to take our sentence upon Himself so we could go free. Therein we see the boundless goodness of God!

And so...

How shall we escape if we neglect so great a salvation, which at the first began to be spoken by the Lord, and was confirmed to us by those who heard Him...

-HEBREWS 2:3

In hell the fire is never quenched, the worms that devour flesh never die, and the people who go there are the living dead. Ever in unspeakable pain and horror, ever remembering, ever tormented, separated forever from God. There is good cause to fear, but...

The fear of the LORD is the beginning of wisdom;
A good understanding have all those who do His commandments.
His praise endures forever.

-PSALM 111:10

*Driven by Eternity:*
## YOUR WEEK IN REVIEW

- Many – even in the church – are unaware of Jesus' teaching about judgment, heaven, and hell.

- The teachings of eternal judgments and rewards are foundational, elementary truths.

- The teachings demand a response. Hell is a real place.

- Jesus was bold and plain and spoke often about hell and judgment because He desires that all would escape hell and be saved.

- Many who claim Jesus as Lord will not enter heaven but will go to hell, because they never really knew and followed Him and His ways.

- It is through the grace of God that we are empowered to follow Christ and His commandments.

There is no need for confusion about this. First John 2:1-6 shows us the simple gospel.

My dear children, *I write this to you so that you will not sin.* But if anybody does sin, we have one who speaks to the Father in our defense – Jesus Christ, the Righteous One. He is the atoning sacrifice for our sins, and not only for ours but also for the sins of the whole world. We know that we have come to know him if we obey his commands. The man who says, "I know him," but does not do what he commands is a liar, and the truth is not in him. But if anyone obeys his word, God's love is truly made complete in him. *This is how we know we are in him: Whoever claims to live in him must walk as Jesus did.*

-NIV, EMPHASIS ADDED

*Matthew Henry's Concise Commentary* puts it this way: "The gospel, when rightly understood and received, sets the heart against all sin, and stops the allowed practice of it; at the same time it gives blessed relief to the wounded consciences of those who have sinned." And so Revelation 22:14 becomes clearer:

Blessed are those who do His commandments, that they may have the right to the tree of life, and may enter through the gates into the city.

Take a look at your journaling from the last six days. Summarize here what God is saying to you this week. Remember God's love, grace and His provision for sin. If the Holy Spirit is pressing upon you, make sure you study and pray through. Don't neglect the salvation God has provided for you. If the Lord is leading you to pray for others, write their names down and pray for them as well.

_____

_____

_____

If there are any specific directions or actions the Lord is leading you to take, record those here. Be sure to follow through on them. Perhaps tell a friend or prayer partner who can pray with you and for you and help you keep your commitments.

_____

_____

_____

IF YOU ARE NOT SURE YOU ARE GOING TO HEAVEN, GO TO APPENDIX A IMMEDIATELY.

*Father, in Jesus' name I come to You now. I bring You all that is on my heart and all that is in my life. I so need You, Lord. I bring my sins to You and place them at the cross. I want to go to heaven. I want to live a lifestyle that pleases You. Forgive me of these sins, Lord, and empower me by Your grace. Fill me with Your Holy Spirit so I may follow You all the days of my life, keeping Your ways, living as a disciple in the midst of a crooked and perverse generation. I want to be one who overcomes to the end, Lord, and I trust You to keep me and hold me as I seek You daily and plant Your Word deeply in my heart.*

*Lord, I ask You to open my heart to hear what the Spirit is saying. In Jesus' name, amen.*

*Then he will say to those on his left, "Depart from me, you who are cursed,*
*into the eternal fire prepared for the devil and his angels."...Then they will go*
*away to eternal punishment, but the righteous to eternal life.*
*-MATTHEW 25:41, 46, NIV*

Eternal judgment, heaven, and hell are basics of God's Word.

**Jonathan Edwards, 1703-1758,** is widely recognized as one of the greatest theologians in American history and in the world. Beginning his college graduate studies at age sixteen, he studied at Yale, and by twenty years old he had received his masters degree. Pastor, author, president of what would become Princeton University, husband to Sarah and father of twelve children, he led one of the most significant revivals of the eighteenth century. Out of a population of 250,000, at least 50,000 were added to the church. It was a revival that affected all of American life – political, social, and intellectual.

At the time Edwards was a pastor in New England, both pulpits and churches were filled with people who were unconverted. Edwards had a great concern for people's souls. It is true he preached sermons full of godly fear and dread, but these primarily contained collections of Scriptures – simply what the Bible had to say on the subject. Of the thousands of pages of sermons he left behind, the majority are about positive biblical themes, such as the peace of the Lord or the comfort of heaven. But his most famous sermon is perhaps "Sinners in the Hands of an Angry God."

Preaching carefully crafted messages with little emotion was Edwards's habit. This sermon had no unusual effect on his congregation, but when he again delivered it as a guest speaker to a church in Enfield, Connecticut, the results were history making.

### The Reality of Hell in the Words of America's Master Preacher

***In the excerpt below, you will find a masterpiece.*** *God's judgments and the reality of hell are portrayed as vividly as anyone has ever done.* Listeners were overwhelmed with an immediate feeling of their peril. Both women and strong men were gripped with awful fear and felt as if they were already slipping into the fires of a lost eternity. They clung to the pillars and chair rails of the building and cried aloud for mercy, looking for something to hold on to, for they felt the floor of the church would suddenly open and swallow them into the fires of hell under their feet. Their terror was so great that it drowned Edwards's voice and he had to ask for silence. Revival then shook Enfield, as it had the rest of the colony.[1]

Consider this, you that are here present, that yet remain in an unregenerate state. That God will execute the fierceness of his anger, implies, that he will inflict wrath without any pity. When God beholds the ineffable extremity of your case, and sees your torment to be so vastly disproportioned to your strength, and sees how your poor soul is crushed, and sinks down, as it were, into an infinite gloom; he will have no compassion upon you, he will not forbear the executions of his wrath, or in the least lighten his hand; there shall be no moderation or mercy, nor will God then at all stay his rough wind; he will have no regard to your welfare, nor be at all careful lest you should suffer too much in any other sense, than only that you shall not suffer beyond what strict justice requires. Nothing shall be withheld, because it is so hard for you to bear. Ezekial.8:18. "Therefore will I also deal in fury: mine eye shall not spare, neither will I have pity; and though they cry in mine ears with a loud voice, yet I will not hear them." Now God stands ready to pity you; this is a day of mercy; you may cry now with some encouragement of obtaining mercy. But when once the day of mercy is past, your most lamentable and dolorous cries and shrieks will be in vain; you will be wholly lost and thrown away of God, as to any regard to your welfare. God will have no other use to put you to, but to suffer misery; you shall be continued in being to no other end; for you will be a vessel of wrath fitted to destruction; and there will be no other use of this vessel, but to be filled full of wrath. God will be so far from pitying you when you cry to him, that it is said he will only "laugh and mock," Proverbs. 1: 25, 26, &c.

Thus it will be with you that are in an unconverted state, if you continue in it; the infinite might, and majesty, and terribleness of the omnipotent God shall be magnified upon you, in the ineffable strength of your torments. You shall be tormented in the presence of the holy angels, and in the presence of the Lamb; and when you shall be in this state of suffering, the glorious inhabitants of heaven shall go forth and look on the awful spectacle, that they may see what the wrath and fierceness of the Almighty is; and when they have seen it, they will fall down and adore that great power and majesty. Isaiah 66: 23, 24. "And it shall come to pass, that from one new moon to another, and from one sabbath to another, shall all flesh come to worship before me, saith the Lord. And they shall go forth and look upon the carcasses of the men that have transgressed against me; for their worm shall not die, neither shall their fire be quenched, and they shall be an abhorring unto all flesh."

It is everlasting wrath. It would be dreadful to suffer this fierceness and wrath of Almighty God one moment; but you must suffer it to all eternity. There will be no end to this exquisite horrible misery. When you look forward, you shall see a long forever, a boundless duration before you, which will swallow up your thoughts, and amaze your soul; and you will absolutely despair of ever having any deliverance, any end, any mitigation, any rest at all. You will know certainly that you must wear out long ages, millions of millions of ages, in wrestling and conflicting with this almighty merciless vengeance; and then when you have so done, when so many ages have actually been spent by you in this manner, you will know that all is but a point to what remains. So that your punishment will indeed be infinite. Oh, who can express what the state of a soul in such circumstances is! All that we can possibly say about it, gives but a very feeble, faint representation of it; it is inexpressible and inconceivable: For "who knows the power of God's anger?"

How dreadful is the state of those that are daily and hourly in the danger of this great wrath and infinite misery! But this is the dismal case of every soul in this congregation that has not been born again, however moral and strict, sober and religious, they may otherwise be. Oh that you would consider it, whether you be young or old! There is reason to think, that there are many in this congregation now hearing this discourse, that will actually be the subjects of this very misery to all eternity. We know not who they are, or in what seats they sit, or what thoughts they now have. It may be they are now at ease, and hear all these things without much disturbance, and are now flattering themselves that they are not the persons, promising themselves that they shall escape. If we knew that there was one person, and but one, in the whole congregation, that was to be the subject of this misery, what an awful thing would it be to think of! If we knew who it was, what an awful sight would it be to see such a person! How might all the rest of the congregation lift up a lamentable and bitter cry over him! But, alas! instead of one, how many is it likely will remember this discourse in hell?

And now you have an extraordinary opportunity, a day wherein Christ has thrown the door of mercy wide open, and stands in calling and crying with a loud voice to poor sinners; a day wherein many are flocking to him, and pressing into the kingdom of God. Many are daily coming from the east, west, north and south; many that were very lately in the same miserable condition that you are in, are now in a happy state, with their hearts filled with love to him who has loved them, and washed them from their sins in his own blood, and rejoicing in hope of the glory of God. How awful is it to be left behind at such a day!

-EXCERPTS FROM "SINNERS IN THE HANDS OF AN ANGRY GOD,"
JULY 8, 1741

1. This was a world-changing sermon that is still impacting lives hundreds of years later! Why do you think this is so?

_____

_____

_____

_____

_____

_____

_____

_____

_____

_____

_____

- How do these very vivid and intensely biblical messages – "Sinners in the Hands of an Angry God" and "Driven by Eternity" – make you feel in your heart and mind?

- Do they lead you to fear hell and believe it is a real place?

- Are your feelings at all similar to those who heard Jonathan Edwards's message in the year 1741?

- What should you do about it? (Did you notice the grace and mercy available in the message?)

Therefore let us go on and get past the elementary stage in the teachings and doctrine of Christ (the Messiah), advancing steadily toward the completeness and perfection that belong to spiritual maturity. Let us not again be laying the foundation of...eternal judgment and punishment. [These are all matters of which you should have been fully aware long, long ago.]

-HEBREWS 6:1-2, AMP

2. Had you ever realized eternal judgment, heaven, and hell were basics of the gospel? Don't say yes too quickly. Be honest and record the difference between what and how you used to believe and what you are learning from the Holy Spirit now:

> *When you understand that everything you do here will be viewed under the scope of His eternal Word and the reward you receive or the loss that you've suffered will endure forever and ever and ever, you'll take notice. I mean I look at people that prepare for retirement, and that's just ten, twenty years, yet they're not preparing for eternity.*
>
> -JOHN BEVERE

3. What practical applications to your daily life do you see when you think about this message and the quote here? Are there changes to your lifestyle or thinking, *or both*, that God is impressing upon you?

_____

_____

_____

_____

## The Question

In Luke 16 the rich man was in Hades, the temporary hell that at the judgment will be cast into the Lake of Fire, which is the eternal hell. (See Revelation 20:11.) When he asks for a miracle to warn his brothers about hell, he is told that the Word of God is enough and nothing more would be given. God knew that if they wouldn't believe the Scriptures, they wouldn't believe a miracle or sign.

That is a very important message for all of us. Miracles and signs may be given to some, according to God's will, who knows everyone's heart. **But the Word of God is what God gives us to convict our hearts and bring us to Himself. The Scriptures are our source of truth about eternity, and God is not required to give anything more. Our response to the Word of God determines where we will spend eternity!**

He answered, "Then I beg you, father, send Lazarus to my father's house, for I have five brothers. Let him warn them, so that they will not also come to this place of torment."

Abraham replied, "They have Moses and the Prophets; let them listen to them."

"No, father Abraham," he said, "but if someone from the dead goes to them, they will repent."

He said to him, "If they do not listen to Moses and the Prophets, they will not be convinced even if someone rises from the dead."

-LUKE 16:27-31, NIV

4. Are you driven by eternity? The word *driven* means to propel; it means to guide, control or direct. What is the driving force behind your life as of right now, and how do you see it stacking up to God's eternal judgment?

_____

_____

_____

_____

## The Answer

The Lake of Fire was not created for human beings but for the devil and his angels (Matt. 25:41).

There is no need to go to hell. Jesus came to give abundant life, not eternal death (John 10:9-10).

At the dawn of the church, Peter faced a crowd who had heard a powerful sermon and who were desperate to find answers. He faced them and boldly proclaimed:

"All Israel, then, know this: There's no longer room for doubt – God made him Master and Messiah, this Jesus whom you killed on a cross."

Cut to the quick, those who were there listening asked Peter and the other apostles, "Brothers! Brothers! So now what do we do?"

Peter said, "Change your life. Turn to God and be baptized, each of you, in the name of Jesus Christ, so your sins are forgiven. Receive the gift of the Holy Spirit. The promise is targeted to you and your children, but also to all who are far away – whomever, in fact, our Master God invites."

He went on in this vein for a long time, urging them over and over, "Get out while you can; get out of this sick and stupid culture!"

That day about three thousand took him at his word, were baptized and were signed up.

-ACTS 2:36-41, THE MESSAGE

IF YOU ARE NOT SURE YOU ARE GOING TO HEAVEN, GO TO APPENDIX A IMMEDIATELY.

**ZENITH**
the time when something is most powerful or successful.

What in this second hour stood out to you the most, and how is it meaningful to your eternal success?

_____

_____

_____

_____

_____

_____

_____

_____

_____

_____

_____

_____

1. Primary sources for biographical sketch: Colin C. Whittaker, Great Revivals (Springfield, MO: Gospel Publishing House, 1986), and Keith J. Hardman, The Spiritual Awakeners (Chicago, IL: Moody Press, 1983).

# *Judgment of Deceived*

## HOUR 3

Please refer to Chapter 5,

Judgment of Deceived,

in the *Driven by Eternity* book

and video session 3.

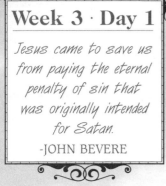

*Jesus came to save us from paying the eternal penalty of sin that was originally intended for Satan.*

-JOHN BEVERE

According to an Ohio State University study, genetic traits passed from crops to their weedy relatives can persist for at least six generations, and probably much longer. This means genetic traits that are developed in crops – such as resistance to insect pests – can become a permanent part of the weed population, in turn posing possible risks to crops.[1] And so a genetic trait can pass from a wonderful and useful plant to a weed and become a permanent part of that weed.

That works as a pretty good analogy for this short devotion. Biblically speaking, Adam's genetic makeup – his nature – is passed on to us, from generation to generation. His fallen nature, his sin is the permanent heritage of all his children, mankind itself. **We are born into Adam's legacy** – and we need to be rescued. But how can a person become wonderfully new, a re-created being with no genetically passed on sin nature?

That is about the same question people asked Jesus in the third chapter of John's Gospel. It is remarkable that no one ever really stops to think about what it means or why it means what it does. Jesus' point is that the only hope of escaping the sin nature with which we're certainly born is to be born...*again*, this time with new "blood," new genetics, a new, pure heritage. Of course a man couldn't reenter his mother's womb and be born all over again. So then what?

Jesus answers in John 3:6-7 (NLT):

> Humans can reproduce only human life, but the Holy Spirit gives new life from heaven. So don't be surprised at my statement that you must be born again.

We have seen over and over that there is a heaven to be gained and a hell to shun. If we have hell's nature – the sin nature – we will naturally be sent there one day. It is who we are and how we have lived in our life.

Our forefather Adam willingly disobeyed God and brought sin upon us all, but Jesus intervened on our behalf.

> This is a faithful saying and worthy of all acceptation, that Christ Jesus came into the world to save sinners.
>
> -1 TIMOTHY 1:15

Only God can offer a new birth and with it a new nature. The new plant will naturally bear good fruit and be gathered in one day with loving care and placed in heaven's garden for eternity.

Have you ever thought about sin, hell, and salvation in this way? Do you live a vital life, born anew of the Holy Spirit, naturally bearing good fruit?

1. "Genes Passed From Crops to Weeds Persist for Generations," Ohio State Research, http://researchnews.osu.edu/archive/rad-weed.htm (accessed January 22, 2006).

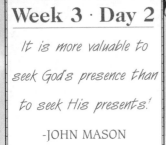

## Week 3 · Day 2

*It is more valuable to seek God's presence than to seek His presents.¹*

-JOHN MASON

I t is a lopsided church that only preaches a gospel of goodness. Even a casual observation of Romans 11:20-23 shows why.

> Because of unbelief they were broken off, and you stand by faith. Do not be haughty, but fear. For if God did not spare the natural branches, He may not spare you either. Therefore consider the goodness and severity of God: on those who fell, severity; but toward you, goodness, if you continue in His goodness. Otherwise you also will be cut off. And they also, if they do not continue in unbelief, will be grafted in, for God is able to graft them in again.

We are plainly told to consider the severity of God along with His goodness. We are not to be haughty or assuming, but we are to fear God, for we see that He does indeed "cut off." And we see this goodness He provides us is something to be "continued in."

Too often we present a God who is more like the genie in Aladdin's lamp or Santa Claus than God the Father Almighty, maker of heaven and earth. God's presence is as a consuming refining fire, burning the dross from the silver and gold. He is as the wind that drives the chaff from the wheat. He is holy, majestic, pure, and righteous. Terrible in His wrath and awesome in His glorious goodness, God is not an idol made in our own image that we can serve as best pleases us.

Continuing in His goodness means we live according to His goodness. Denying fleshly lusts, taking up our cross, we are empowered divinely by Jesus, in the Holy Spirit, as children of our Father God! Jesus tells us in John 14:21 that if we love Him, we will keep His commandments. **So if we do not keep His commandments, what does that mean?**

> You will know them by their fruits. Do men gather grapes from thorn-bushes or figs from thistles? Even so, every good tree bears good fruit, but a bad tree bears bad fruit. A good tree cannot bear bad fruit, nor can a bad tree bear good fruit. Every tree that does not bear good fruit is cut down and thrown into the fire. Therefore by their fruits you will know them.
>
> -MATTHEW 7:16-20

Go back to John 14:21. The last part reads, "And he who loves Me will be loved by My Father, and I will love him and manifest Myself to him."

The presence of Jesus in our lives is what gives us the power to continue in His goodness. We must love Him in word, in deed, and in character as well as by association. We must seek the Giver Himself, not just the gifts He provides.

> Establish Your word to Your servant, who is devoted to fearing You.
>
> -PSALM 119:38

On the lines below, ask God for His presence in your life to empower you for a lifestyle of bearing good fruit.

1. John Mason, *An Enemy Called Average* (Colorado Springs, CO: Cook Communications Ministries, 2003), 107.

# Week 3 · Day 3

*The really good news for Christians is that Jesus is now taking students in the master class of life...So the message of and about him is specifically a gospel for our life now, not just for dying. It is about living now as his apprentice in kingdom living, not just as a consumer of his merits.*

-DALLAS WILLARD

iscipleship is sometimes seen as a nasty word. Or a legalistic term. This is a sad development in today's world. What could be more beautiful to a real Christian than to look like his Master? **What could be more exciting, more exhilarating than to be invited to be...*HIS* DISCIPLE?**

Being "saved" is about so much more than a one-time prayer to go to heaven. So called "fire insurance" mentality is no way to get you there anyway. What is the motive behind your following this one you call Lord?

Judas spent a lot of time with Jesus. He was a prime player. Attending the Lord's classes, attending to the Lord's needs, and attending ultimately to his own agenda. Judas's heart was revealed in the end to be far from Christ, far from God, regardless of how he ministered to the crowds. Yet even the fellow disciples who walked and worked alongside Judas daily hadn't a clue there was an imposter among them.

But Jesus knew. And He knows today who is with Him in words only but not deeds. And even then, let us remember that Judas was very busy with "kingdom business"! Why, it appeared to others he had faith and plenty of good works as well.

*Appeared* is the key word here. In truth, Judas' intentions were not right from the start. He was self-seeking, a liar, and a flatterer. A thief, he even took money from Jesus' ministry. All this while working "in the ministry."

We can fool people if we work hard enough. We can even fool ourselves, which is a scary thought. How do we know? We need to let God's Word tell us how we should live. If our heart is deceived, it will show up in our deeds sooner or later.

"Not by might nor by power, but by My Spirit," says the LORD of hosts.
-ZECHARIAH 4:6

Rather than fearing the discipline of discipleship, we should embrace the glory of union with God by His Spirit. He will lead us and guide in the ways we should go. He will grace us and bless us as we follow His lead to heaven. As we place ourselves in His hands, He is faithful and just, not only to cleanse us from sin, but also to keep us on His path.

## PRAYER OF DISCIPLESHIP

*Lord, I want to enter Your school of discipleship. I desire to be driven by eternity, not by self or by the world's influences. I cannot do it on my own, but I can and do choose daily to serve You and to follow Your Word in all I do. I want a lifestyle that is born of my relationship with You, Lord. Teach me, lead me, guide me, and empower me. Help me understand Your Word. I seek You now, Lord. Open the eyes of my heart that I may know You and remain in You and be Your disciple.*

1. Dallas Willard, *The Divine Conspiracy* (San Francisco: HarperSanFrancisco, 1998), xvii.

# Week 3 · Day 4

*We've preached a gospel that speaks of a free salvation, which is absolutely accurate, but we've neglected to tell candidates it would cost them their freedom. When I speak of freedom, it isn't real, but perceived liberty, for all those outside of Christ are bound to sin. They are slaves even though they may fully believe they're free.*

-JOHN BEVERE

**S**tatistics reveal the lie of today's "freedoms." Most women who have an abortion are tormented by their decision – sometimes for a lifetime. Ask someone who kills an innocent family in a drunken car accident if it was great to get "loaded." Ask the junkie how cool it is to stay "high" all the time. Ask the children of the divorced parents or the victim of adultery or pornography or AIDS if the sexual "freedom" was worth it.

It's bewildering that we continue to champion freedoms that are so obviously tearing us apart. Holiness isn't just godly; it's also healthy! It's no surprise that God knows what is best for us. But oh, we love to go our own way!

> For, brethren, ye have been called unto liberty; only use not liberty for an occasion to the flesh, but by love serve one another.
> -GALATIANS 5:13, KJV

Our version of freedom is one thing, and it so often leads to pain. God's definition is quite another. Even then, we are prone to use the liberty God does afford us – which is vast – in the wrong ways. Rather than walking in the discipline of His Spirit and Word, we often attempt to continue a lifestyle of self and the flesh. Author John Mason calls that "one foot in the world, one foot in heaven."[1]

That is a very suspect situation for someone who calls themselves a believer and follower of Christ.

Living according to our selfish desires and fleshly lusts doesn't demonstrate love to one another. It only brings hurt. How do we reconcile our actions when we compare them to esteeming one another and loving one another?

If it doesn't "look like Jesus," you probably shouldn't be doing it. **If you couldn't do it with Jesus in the room, your act of "freedom" is slavery and sin.** The giving up of the worldly so-called freedoms that the gospel asks (demands, really) is the best thing that could ever happen to you – now and for the life to come.

Taste and see that the Lord is good. You will not be disappointed when you experience the feeling of the true, clean, refreshing, pure freedom that comes when you give your *whole* self to Christ.

### PRAYER
*Father, Jesus made me free from the law of sin and death, and gave me a new definition of freedom. Help me live worthy of that calling. Show me what freedom in You truly looks like in real life as I seek You in Your Word. In Jesus' name, amen.*

Are there some "freedoms" you practice that the Holy Spirit wants to shed His light on? Is there some slavery or bondage the Lord can set you free from right now? Ask Him in prayer.

1. John Mason, *Let Go of Whatever Makes You Stop* (Tulsa, OK: Insight Publishing Group, 1994), 109.

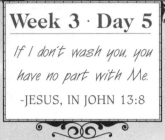

Jesus warned people because He loved them. Here the Master of all washes the disciples' feet. He is teaching them by example about salvation, servanthood, and holiness. It's a strong rebuke and warning to all. *"If I don't wash you, you have no part with Me."*

Among these was Judas. He certainly looked as if he were fulfilling God's call. But Jesus knew the difference between appearances and the true motives of the heart. Judas's heart had become soiled and unclean (v. 11).

> If you know these things, blessed are you if you do them.
>
> -JOHN 13:17

Judas had long ago stopped "doing" the words of Jesus. Those who have a part with Jesus are washed by His words. Obedience proves our "cleanliness".

> …just as Christ also loved the church and gave Himself for her, that He might sanctify and cleanse her with the washing of water by the word, that He might present her to Himself a glorious church, not having spot or wrinkle or any such thing, but that she should be holy and without blemish.
>
> -EPHESIANS 5:25-27

Paul followed Jesus' example as both a servant and a teacher.

> Therefore watch, and remember, that by the space of three years I ceased not to warn every one night and day with tears. And now, brethren, I commend you to God, and to the word of his grace, which is able to build you up, and to give you an inheritance among all them which are sanctified.
>
> -ACTS 20:31-32, KJV

Paul for three years is passionately warning and teaching about grace. *Matthew Henry's Concise Commentary* says this about Paul's words: "Paul directs them to look up to God with faith, and commends them to the word of God's grace, not only as the foundation of their hope and the fountain of their joy, but as the rule of their walking."[1]

Through God's grace you are freely saved, and through that same Word you must find your rule of daily living. It's one thing to know these things…it is quite another to *do* them.

It wasn't just for the disciples these things were said. It was also for us. You have no part with Jesus unless He's washed you, by His blood, by the water of His Word. **You can't call yourself a follower of Jesus but not do the things Jesus said.** Let Him wash you now, by His Word, as He speaks to you about this very thing. What is He saying?

_____

_____

_____

1. Matthew Henry, *Matthew Henry's Concise Commentary on the Whole Bible* (Nashville, TN: Nelson Reference, 2000).

## Week 3 · Day 6

*As those cannot be welcome guests to the Holy God who are unsanctified; so heaven would be no heaven to them; but to all who are born again, and in whom the image of God is renewed, it is sure, as almighty power and eternal truth make it so.*

-MATTHEW HENRY'S CONCISE COMMENTARY (ACTS 20:31-32)

We all want one day to hear Jesus say, "Well done, good and faithful servant" (Matt. 25:21). But it is interesting to note the verse doesn't say, "*Well prayed*, good and faithful servant." Or well *thought*. Or well *imagined*. Or well *intentioned*.

No, it says well *done*, which means you have to DO something.

What do you have to do? Obey. Obey His words, His teachings, His will. Jesus is talking about stewardship, **accountability for the way you have lived your life**. That is hardly a popular subject, in today's Western culture especially. **Nonetheless we will all be called to account for our lifestyle and the things it did or didn't produce**. Every word, every deed, every thought, every intent.

Theologian and scholar Dallas Willard speaks of barcode faith.[1] We'll borrow just a bit from his concept here. Once a product is given a barcode, there is nothing more to be done. From shipping by the manufacturer to the inventory in the store, to the final customer at checkout, it is totally accounted for. No matter what the product is or does, it is recognized by the scanner; it is recorded once for all. In the same way, many believers imagine if they've once prayed the "sinner's prayer" or walked down the aisle of some church or crusade, they've in essence been given their barcode by God, and nothing else is required from there on out. When it comes to the "checkout" line of death for heaven's entrance, they're all set. God will simply "scan" them, and all is well, regardless of what they are or have done.

Willard points out that this is hardly a biblical concept. Believing with your heart and saying with your mouth Jesus is Lord, as Romans 10:9-10 states, is great. Yet it is certainly not the end of the story. The rest of the believing and saying is the doing. If you are a Christian, you'll look like a Christian. You'll live like a Christian. But not because of some strict set of rules or laws or uptight standard of so-called holiness. You will do so because the Holy Spirit in you brings Christ's nature to you. And when you take on His nature, of course, you will grow in His characteristics. Perfectly, without fail? No.

> But we have this treasure in earthen vessels, that the excellence of the power may be of God and not of us. We are hard-pressed on every side, yet not crushed; we are perplexed, but not in despair; persecuted, but not forsaken; struck down, but not destroyed – always carrying about in the body the dying of the Lord Jesus, that the life of Jesus also may be manifested in our body.
>
> -2 CORINTHIANS 4:7-10

We are going to make mistakes. The "doing" is in the living, living like the One we claim is our Lord. We find HOW to do this and WHAT it looks like in His Word. We cannot do it by ourselves – we are but God-breathed earth. Dust. But we do have daily choices, and we have no excuses. Christ in us is our hope of glory (Col. 1:27), and if He's in there, you'll start to show it by what you do and don't do. **Christians in the early church were substantively and markedly different from those who didn't call Jesus Lord. Christianity can be no other way today, by its very nature.**

What is the evidence in your own life that you have had a true nature change?

1. Dallas Willard, *The Divine Conspiracy* (San Francisco: HarperSanFrancisco, 1998).

## Week 3 · Day 7

*Jesus promises eternal reward for those who prove worthy of his trust.*

-MATTHEW HENRY'S CONCISE COMMENTARY (MATTHEW 25:21)

We're saying it again because it is the point that must be made. The "against the grain" message of Jesus Christ was and is that of 2 Corinthians 5:17: "Therefore, if anyone is in Christ, he is a new creation; old things have passed away; behold, all things have become new."

Many today desperately want that verse to mean that if anyone has once prayed a prayer or told their friends they love Jesus or had an experience with Jesus, they have once for all become new; nothing more to it than that. But while it is indeed true that when a person becomes born again, washed in the blood sacrifice of Christ and regenerated, they do become new, it is also an inseparable fact that their new nature will produce conviction of sin, desire for a holy walk with God, and ultimately a changed life. A life for all to see, translated from the kingdom of darkness into the kingdom of light, from satanic and selfish ways to God's ways. **Far from just claiming it, if you are truly a "new creation," it will show**. Some show it more than others, but how can it not show, if it is reality?

Nicodemus, a religious leader who was afraid to be seen with Christ, came to Jesus under the cover of darkness and was told no one can see the kingdom of God unless they are born again. He was received by a loving Jesus under the cover of nighttime, but later Nicodemus takes his faith to the daylight. After Jesus was crucified, Nicodemus helped Joseph of Arimathea in preparing Jesus' body for burial. Christ calls us while we are yet in the darkness, but He calls us to walk in the light as He is in the light. "But if we walk in the light, as he is in the light, we have fellowship with one another, and the blood of Jesus, his Son, purifies us from all sin" (1 John 1:7, NIV).

> Don't love the world's ways. Don't love the world's goods. Love of the world squeezes out love for the Father. Practically everything that goes on in the world – wanting your own way, wanting everything for yourself, wanting to appear important – has nothing to do with the Father. It just isolates you from him. The world and all its wanting, wanting, wanting is on the way out – *but whoever does what God wants is set for eternity*.
> -1 JOHN 2:15-17, THE MESSAGE, EMPHASIS ADDED

If we are truly saved, we are born from the spiritual womb; we will desire the milk of the Word. Then we will grow up to eat solid food (Heb. 5:13; 1 Pet. 2:2). Others who are saved and those who are not will see the fruit of a genuine new birth.

> Command and teach these things. Don't let anyone look down on you because you are young, but set an example for the believers in speech, in life, in love, in faith and in purity.
> -1 TIMOTHY 4:11-12, NIV

Our life will be an example in our words, in our way of daily living, and in our love, faith, and purity. These are not just nice religious things to say, meant to be used in poetry or for ministers only. They are truth by which all will be judged and rewarded accordingly. We either enter with our new family to heaven, or we are forever committed to hell as part of our original earthly, unregenerate family.

*Driven by Eternity:*
## YOUR WEEK IN REVIEW

- We are born Adam's descendants. We need to be rescued from sin's destination, which is hell.

- Jesus came to rescue us. How will we respond?

- If we love Him, we will keep His commands. We will be His disciples.

- Statistics demonstrate that the world's "freedoms" can be terrible bondage and pain.

- Blessed and truly free are those who do Jesus' sayings.

- God holds us accountable for our lifestyle and what it produces.

- By their very nature, Christians are going to be markedly different from those who are not. And each ends up among their own family in eternity, heaven or hell.

Take a look at your journaling from the last six days. Summarize here what God is saying to you this week. **Does your life prove the reality of a new birth?**

_____

_____

Are there any specific directions or actions the Lord is leading you to take?

_____

_____

### THE WEEK IN PRAYER

*Father, in Jesus' name I pray. I come to You and ask You to search my heart and my ways. I desire to be found in You. I desire to serve You in the light. I want to be a disciple, a true believer whose life demonstrates the nature and fruit of one who was born from heaven, born again, delivered from the darkness and birthed into the light; from the kingdom of Satan to the kingdom of Your dear Son, Jesus, who is the Christ.*

*Lord, only the grace of God in me can bring me to You and keep me in You. I pray Your Word, this benediction prayer from the Book of Hebrews, chapter 13, verses 20 and 21:*

*"Now may the God of peace who brought up our Lord Jesus from the dead, that great Shepherd of the sheep, through the blood of the everlasting covenant, make you complete in every good work to do His will, working in you what is well pleasing in His sight, through Jesus Christ, to whom be glory forever and ever."*

*Father God, I pray this for myself – I need You, Lord – make me complete in every good work to do Your will. Work in me what is well pleasing in Your sight, through Jesus Christ. I commit my lifestyle to You, and I trust You to bring me home as I choose to follow You daily. To You, Lord, be glory forever and ever. Amen.*

Knowing the correct password – saying "Master, Master," for instance – isn't going to get you anywhere with me. What is required is serious obedience – doing what my Father wills. I can see it now – at the Final Judgment thousands strutting up to me and saying, "Master, we preached the Message, we bashed the demons, our God-sponsored projects had everyone talking." And do you know what I am going to say? "You missed the boat. All you did was use me to make yourselves important. You don't impress me one bit. You're out of here."

These words I speak to you are not incidental additions to your life, homeowner improvements to your standard of living. They are foundational words, words to build a life on. If you work these words into your life, you are like a smart carpenter who built his house on solid rock. Rain poured down, the river flooded, a tornado hit – but nothing moved that house. It was fixed to the rock.

But if you just use my words in Bible studies and don't work them into your life, you are like a stupid carpenter who built his house on the sandy beach. When a storm rolled in and the waves came up, it collapsed like a house of cards.

-MATTHEW 7:21-27, THE MESSAGE

Not everyone who calls Jesus "Lord" will enter heaven. Only those with a changed nature – the nature of Christ.

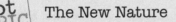 **The New Nature**

Have you ever thought about the fact that if Christ has given the Christian a new nature, the new nature will be evident? Does your lifestyle show the new DNA?

1. What was the most challenging part in this hour of *Driven by Eternity*?

2. Why was that so difficult?

3. What challenges are you experiencing in your own life, right now, that are being affected by this message?

Remember the story about the person who joins the military because the advertisements look so "cool," so adventurous, romantic and exciting.

If you have "joined up" with Jesus and didn't really understand what it was all about, you are not alone. But like the person who gets the shock of his or her life upon entering basic training and then going into the brutal action of war, you can make the decision to get your heart right – and by God's grace move forward in faith!

4. There is a big difference between the born again club and truly following Jesus. Did you receive Jesus and then realize it was more than you bargained for?

5. What have been some of these challenges?

6. How are you now living in God's empowering grace, bearing the fruit of a biblical lifestyle?

**ZENITH**
the time when
something is
most powerful
or successful.

What one primary truth can you take away from this third hour? How is it meaningful to your eternal success?

The Great Falling Away

HOUR 4

Please refer to Chapter 6,

The Great Falling Away,

in the *Driven by Eternity* book

and video session 4.

## Week 4 · Day 1

*If you would follow
on to know the Lord,
come at once to the
open Bible expecting
it to speak to you.
Do not come with the
notion that it is a
thing which you may
push around at your
convenience.*

-A.W. TOZER

When we open our Bibles, do we read what we believe, or do we believe what we read? Think about the difference. Depending on what school of thought we come from, it is a natural tendency to read the Bible – and almost everything – through those glasses.

Are you reading through the eyes of some great Bible teacher or scholar...or of the worldly, sophisticated pagan...or the view from a religious order? Or are you letting the Holy Spirit be your eyes and ears, simply letting the Word speak for itself? It is a topic worthy of consideration. *Don't go through your whole life filtering God's truth through someone else's understanding!*

God gave Bible teachers, pastors, writers, and such for our benefit! And we must learn from them. We are to be involved and closely knit with our local fellowship of believers who can help us in the things of God. But ultimately we stand alone before God at the judgment. If we rely on anything other than Christ's Word, we are in danger. We won't be able to say, "But so-and-so said such-and-such," and then hope to be "let off."

So what must we do? Read the Bible for yourself, be a person of serious prayer, and stay involved in your local Bible-believing church! Ask God to lead you and teach you in His ways. Here are some verses to help:

Study to shew thyself approved unto God, a workman that needeth not to be ashamed, rightly dividing the word of truth.

-2 TIMOTHY 2:15, KJV

But the Helper, the Holy Spirit, whom the Father will send in My name, He will teach you all things, and bring to your remembrance all things that I said to you.

-JOHN 14:26

God means what he says. What he says goes. His powerful Word is sharp as a surgeon's scalpel, cutting through everything, whether doubt or defense, laying us open to listen and obey.

-HEBREWS 4:12, THE MESSAGE

Trust in the LORD with all your heart, and lean not on your own understanding; in all your ways acknowledge Him, and He shall direct your paths.

-PROVERBS 3:5-6

Make today special. Take these Scriptures to prayer, and in faith ask God to open your eyes to His Word concerning the subjects of heaven, hell, and eternity. Journal your thoughts on the next page.

1. A. W. Tozer, *The Pursuit of God* (N.p.: Christian Publications, 1994), chapter 6, "The Speaking Voice."

## Week 4 · Day 2

*If your name is going to be erased from the Book of Life, what does that mean? It had to have been in there. "Blotted out" means you had to be at one time written in.*

-JOHN BEVERE

The Scriptures speak of some who may actually have their names removed from the Book of Life! People who at one time were reason for the angels to rejoice become cause for sorrow, having their names blotted out. Those who remain faithful to His Word – their names will remain in that sacred record. And to have your name recorded in the Lamb's Book of Life means untold joy for eternity.

> Thus shall he who conquers (is victorious) be clad in white garments, and I will not erase or blot out his name from the Book of Life; I will acknowledge him [as Mine] and I will confess his name openly before My Father and before His angels. He who is able to hear, let him listen to and heed what the [Holy] Spirit says to the assemblies (churches).
>
> -REVELATION 3:5-6, AMP

We live in an age where we can easily get thousands of opinions on nearly any subject. Television, newspapers, huge state-of-the-art libraries, "gourmet" bookstores with mega media departments, and countless newsletters, magazines, and direct mailings bring us all the information we might want. And if you have Internet access, you can find massive amounts of information on nearly any topic you could imagine within seconds.

All of that can be great, but thank God we have the Word of God! Rather than being tossed about by a thousand different voices, we can simply turn to the Bible as our ultimate source of truth and comfort. Jesus reveals to us the way to live a life driven by eternity, as opposed to a life driven by every voice of the world's intrusive mass media and ever-increasing information.

The Book of Revelation actually begins with these words: *"The Revelation of Jesus Christ."* It tells us of Jesus, the One who captures our hearts, whose eyes are flames of fire and feet as polished brass; the Sovereign King who speaks to us in the things that render us speechless – the awe-inspiring wonders of nature, the matchless poetry and power of His Word, and the loving comfort of His Spirit. Who is like the King of glory? No one, and His children know it to be true.

There is only one way, one truth, and one life – and that is Jesus Christ. **As you follow Him, staying faithful to His Word, you will endure to the end and your name will be found in the Book of Life.**

Are you living a life that is faithful to Christ and His ways as revealed in the Word of God? If not, what can you do to do so?

## Week 4 · Day 3

*Don't worry about what you do not understand...Worry about what you do understand in the Bible but do not live by.*

-CORRIE TEN BOOM

Jesus came as a humble carpenter's son. He ministered among the common people in everyday ways teaching in field and mountain, along the way as He traveled, and in synagogues. He gave Himself to all people – those of the past, to us today, and to His followers in the future. The Old Testament, which Jesus often quoted, and the New Testament are the Word of God, which is His message for everyone. A book to understand, to live by, and to share with others, the Bible is at once historic, contemporary, and eternal.

There are nearly 800,000 words in the King James Version.[1] It contains 66 books of history, genealogies, letters, prophecy, poetry, songs, and much more. It is full of practical truths you can live by each day as you reach toward eternity. Depending on the particular version you read, there are approximately 1189 chapters, with more than 31,000 verses. It is the world's all-time best seller and most translated and enduring work.

With all the ideas, philosophies, and knowledge available in the world, many people give endless reasons as to why they believe or do little or nothing concerning things of faith. Many throw their hands up in confusion or exasperation. "After all," they say, "the Bible is only one voice among countless others in our modern age. And anyway," they cry, "how can we understand it? How can we know it is truth?" But these excuses will not be accepted by God. He has given the ultimate Teacher, the Holy Spirit (Luke 11:13, John 14:26), to those who will but ask. Further, many Scriptures tell us we have a responsibility to study and understand God's Word and that God will illuminate it to us as we seek Him.

Perhaps you do not understand some things in the Word of God, but the real issue is, are you living what you *do* know?

1. About the Bible, ChristianAnswers.net, http://www.christiananswers.net/bible/about.html (accessed February 4, 2006).

## Week 4 · Day 4

*I believe that the Bible is to be understood and received in the plain and obvious meaning of its passages; since I cannot persuade myself that a book intended for the instruction and conversion of the whole world, should cover its true meaning in such mystery and doubt, that none but critics and philosophers can discover it.*

-DANIEL WEBSTER

Thank God the Bible is written for all of us and is available today in plain language. Each of us can understand it if we simply read it and believe it, trusting the Holy Spirit. Paul wrote to Timothy, who was growing in his role as a pastor, a straightforward and clear warning: "Now the Spirit expressly says that in latter times some will depart from the faith" (1 Tim. 4:1). Notice that he stated that the Spirit speaks *expressly*. That means this is a definite fact and you need to pay close attention.

Paul also said that "some will depart from the faith." If he says they will depart from the faith, that means they were once *in* the faith. You have to actually be in something to depart from it.

Paul's warning continues:

...giving heed to seducing spirits, and doctrines of devils; speaking lies in hypocrisy; having their conscience seared with a hot iron.

-1 TIMOTHY 4:1-2, KJV

This passage does not say these people were never Christians to begin with. It doesn't say they only *claimed* to be Christians but were not. In fact, the point of the chapter is that there will be those who have departed from among us and will then teach wrong doctrine, and we are to beware of them! Like wolves in sheep's clothing, these are a danger to the flock. They have rejected the Lord's ways, and their hearts have become "seared" because they gave heed to seducing spirits and doctrines of devils. They may look religious, as though they still are in the faith, but they are not.

Remember Judas? One of the twelve chosen, serving alongside Jesus, working miracles and in the ministry for years, yet he steals, lies, betrays, and ultimately is lost (John 17:12). He began in the faith but departed from it, *permanently* rejecting Christ.

*You won't depart from the faith if you keep your heart humble and conscience clean by the Word and Spirit.*

How is your conscience? Are there things in your life trying to lead you from the faith? What are they?

_____

_____

_____

_____

_____

1. Daniel Webster, speech given at Bunker Hill Monument, Charleston, Massachusetts, June 17, 1843.

## Week 4 · Day 5

*Jesus said, "I will never leave you nor forsake you," but He never said that we can't leave or forsake Him.*

-JOHN BEVERE

To live a life driven by eternity means peace for your heart and grace to meet life's challenges. It is a life that brings fulfillment to your deepest needs and blessings to others. Putting God's will first bears fruit in this life and in the life to come. But unfortunately, this is not the way most people live. Driven by today's needs and desires, few think of much beyond tomorrow. Many say they are "too busy," or they "hope it will all pan out." There are plenty of reasons people give for not coming to terms with eternity. Since it is something we all will face, you would think everyone would be doing some serious soul searching!

But if our gospel be hid, it is hid to them that are lost: in whom the god of this world hath blinded the minds of them which believe not, lest the light of the glorious gospel of Christ, who is the image of God, should shine unto them.

-2 CORINTHIANS 4:3-4, KJV

In those verses we find some answers. Satan has clouded the reality of eternity. From the time of Adam and Eve to this day he veils the truth, mixes it, perverts it, and changes it to lies. This is the reason multitudes inside and outside of the church never think clearly about eternity.

For those who don't know the Lord, we must pray, believe, and witness to them in power. For the church, God calls each of us to the glories of walking with Him in obedience. That is how you live a life driven by eternity. But obedience seems to be a relic or an unattainable ideal to most. Pop culture today says, "Even if God were real and you could intimately know Him, it is all relative: *however you want to interpret it* or *whatever works for you* is good and right, *as long as nobody else gets hurt*." Tragically, even many in the church buy into that lie and risk eternity itself. "I'm a believer, I have needs, and God's grace covers all my sins" is a common excuse for a disobedient life. While God's grace *is* sufficient and He will not forsake us, He is also holy, majestic, and just. He knows when He is being "played the fool."

Rather than forsaking the call to watch and pray, to be holy as He is holy, and to contend for the faith, you are to follow God's ways. **You have been saved for a purpose, to make an impact on eternity.** You must be obedient to all His ways by the power of the Holy Spirit.

Do not be deceived: God cannot be mocked. A man reaps what he sows. The one who sows to please his sinful nature, from that nature will reap destruction; the one who sows to please the Spirit, from the Spirit will reap eternal life.

-GALATIANS 6:7-8, NIV

Those who sow to the Spirit are driven by eternity. Sowing to please the sinful nature is forsaking the things of eternity. To which are you sowing? How can the Holy Spirit help you today?

## Week 4 · Day 6

*Therefore let him who thinks he stands take heed lest he fall.*

-THE APOSTLE PAUL, 1 CORINTHIANS 10:12

ccording to the *Chicago Tribune*, on Monday, February 6, 1995, a Detroit bus driver finished his shift and on the way back to the terminal made a wrong turn. His supervisors began looking for him. His wife called and reported that her husband might be disoriented from medication he was taking. Six hours later the huge bus and driver were found two hundred miles from Detroit. Slowly weaving from side to side down a rural road, he was pulled over by state police. The driver had no idea where he was and agreed he had made a wrong turn somewhere.[1]

In today's fast-paced world, money, sex, fame, information, and technology seem to rule society. Relativism and self-seeking are very much the standard, and there are endless voices vying for our attention. It is easy to be wandering or even lost in the midst of it all. *It is possible to start out right, yet wander off the path and be lost, never finding our way back home.* We may be slightly or severely off course and only dimly aware of it if at all.

For one who believes Jesus Christ is Lord, it is a given that she or he is called upon to run the race, guard their heart, and finish well. Living as a so-called nominal or marginal Christian is not an option. Living a lifestyle contrary to God's Word, dependent upon a hope that you can do as you please with your life and at the end Jesus won't "forsake" you hardly seems to fit with any genuine biblical example. There clearly is more to salvation than what is generally popularly presented. Even a one-time reading of the Bible reveals that a quick prayer, a baptism, or a walk down the church aisle isn't all there is to genuine saving faith and what a Christian's life is and looks like.

Is there "eternal security"? Surely Jesus will never leave or forsake the believer. But we may leave Him, and for those who desire to play around the edges, here is some food for thought. Scripture speaks loudly about the difference between starting and finishing in the faith:

*If* we endure, we will also reign with him. *If we disown him, he will also disown us.*
-2 TIMOTHY 2:12, NIV, EMPHASIS ADDED

But exhort one another daily, while it is called "today"; lest any of you be hardened through the deceitfulness of sin. *For we have become partakers of Christ, if we hold the beginning of our confidence stedfast unto the end.*
-HEBREWS 3:13-14, EMPHASIS ADDED

Now, brothers, I want to remind you of the gospel I preached to you, which you received and on which you have taken your stand. By this gospel you are saved, *if you hold firmly to the word I preached to you. Otherwise, you have believed in vain.*
-1 CORINTHIANS 15:1-2, NIV, EMPHASIS ADDED

**For today's prayer and journaling, simply follow the Word of God:** "Examine yourselves to see whether you are in the faith; test yourselves. Do you not realize that Christ Jesus is in you – unless, of course, you fail the test?" (2 Cor. 13:5, NIV).

Journal here what God reveals to you.

1. "Mixed-up Bus Driver From Motor City Ends Day Near Mackinac," *Chicago Tribune*, February 8, 1995, in *Contemporary Illustrations for Preachers, Teachers and Writers*, ed. Craig Larson (Grand Rapids, MI: Baker Books), 12.

## Week 4 · Day 7

*I've had several people come up to me in the past in tears saying that they at one time told the Lord they didn't want to serve Him any longer. Later they felt deep remorse and repented. They experienced great fear when encountering Scripture... in their Bibles. To...comfort these troubled souls, I tell them if they did commit the sin unto death they wouldn't have a desire to come back into sweet fellowship with Jesus. The very fact they hungered for Him and did indeed repent, accompanied by godly fruit, meant the Holy Spirit drew them back into fellowship.*

-JOHN BEVERE

We have discovered that the message of "falling from grace" – that it is possible to permanently depart from the faith, becoming "twice dead" (Jude 12) and therefore be condemned to hell – is straight from Scripture and part of our "solid foundation" in Christ. The healthy fear of God – reverential love and respect – is very different from being scared of God, and it helps us stay on the straight and narrow. God has empowered us by His grace to follow Him because we love Him and want to please Him as our heavenly Father. If we sin, our hearts will be smitten by the Holy Spirit, and God will give us true repentance and forgive us.

This is not a message of legalism or fear tactics. It is simply the biblical message that if we love Him, we will keep His commandments. Otherwise we are deceiving ourselves and others. We must be born again, and we must – by His empowering grace – keep ourselves in the love of God. Let's look at some Scriptures that state this very plainly.

But in keeping with his promise we are looking forward to a new heaven and a new earth, the home of righteousness. So then, dear friends, since you are looking forward to this, make every effort to be found spotless, blameless and at peace with him....Therefore, dear friends, since you already know this, *be on your guard so that you may not be carried away by the error of lawless men and fall from your secure position. But grow in the grace and knowledge of our Lord and Savior Jesus Christ.*
-2 PETER 3:13-18, NIV, EMPHASIS ADDED

If we say that we have fellowship with Him, and walk in darkness, we lie and do not practice the truth. But if we walk in the light as He is in the light, we have fellowship with one another, and the blood of Jesus Christ His Son cleanses us from all sin. If we say that we have no sin, we deceive ourselves, and the truth is not in us. If we confess our sins, He is faithful and just to forgive us our sins and to cleanse us from all unrighteousness. If we say that we have not sinned, we make Him a liar, and His word is not in us.

*My little children, these things I write to you, so that you may not sin.* And *if anyone sins, we have an Advocate with the Father, Jesus Christ the righteous. And He Himself is the propitiation for our sins, and not for ours only but also for the whole world. Now by this we know that we know Him, if we keep His command-ments. He who says, "I know Him," and does not keep His commandments, is a liar, and the truth is not in him.* But whoever keeps His word, truly the love of God

is perfected in him. By this we know that we are in Him. *He who says he abides in Him ought himself also to walk just as He walked. Brethren, I write no new commandment to you, but an old commandment which you have had from the beginning.*
-1 JOHN 1:6-2:7, EMPHASIS ADDED

God has given you His grace, which empowers you to love and follow Him according to His Word and to be strong to the end.

First Corinthians 1:8 says, "He will keep you strong to the end, so that you will be blameless on the day of our Lord Jesus Christ" (NIV).

In the Book of Jude, we see how to keep our love for God fresh, even if there is sin and apostasy in the church. Verses 20 and 21 (KJV) read:

But ye, beloved, building up yourselves on your most holy faith, praying in the Holy Ghost, keep yourselves in the love of God, looking for the mercy of our Lord Jesus Christ unto eternal life.

**What brings us home to God?** By His power and His grace, we look for the mercy and the coming of the Lord every moment of the day. (Remember in the Gospels – the servant who fell away was the one who wasn't anticipating the return of his master [Luke 12:45-46].) We are to long for Him and seek Him continually, for "everyone who has this hope in Him *purifies* himself, just as He is pure" (1 John 3:3, emphasis added). We are to keep ourselves in the love of God, by the power of His Spirit, obeying Him because we love Him. *Not only will the Holy Spirit within us confirm that we are God's children, but our daily lifestyle will also witness to our heart and to the world that we are His children!*

The Bible is clear: your beloved Jesus is able to keep you from stumbling.

Now unto him that is able to keep you from falling, and to present you faultless before the presence of his glory with exceeding joy, to the only wise God our Saviour, be glory and majesty, dominion and power, both now and ever. Amen.
-JUDE 24-25, KJV

*Driven by Eternity:*
## YOUR WEEK IN REVIEW

Look at the brief review below.
- When it comes to the Bible, believe what you read; don't read what you believe.

    He who overcomes shall be clothed in white garments, and I will not blot out his name from the Book of Life.
    -REVELATION 3:5

- Do the things – the basics of the faith – that you understand. Meanwhile, trust God to reveal more to you.

- Is there anything in your life you are risking eternity for?

- When we get off course, we may hardly even know it. We need God to keep us on track.

Your eternal well-being is worth the time to sort out what God is saying to you this week. Pray, journal and follow through on how God is leading you.

## THE WEEK IN PRAYER

*O Father God, in Jesus' name I pray. I do fear You – but not because I am scared of You. Rather, I love and respect You as a father – as my Father: majestic, holy, almighty God. The One I can trust to love and care for me, to protect me, to chastise me for my own well-being when I do wrong, to tell me what and how to do right, to give me all the grace I need daily so ultimately I can come home to live with You forever in heaven.*

*Lord, I come boldly to the throne of grace that I may obtain mercy and find grace to help in time of need. I confess any and all sin to you now.* [Confess any sin and repent. If you have a recurring lifestyle of sin or "addiction," get some help from qualified professionals and your local church! Don't wait; seek the Lord while He may be found and then continue in His love, His forgiveness, and His Word.]

*Lord, You are faithful and just to forgive me and to cleanse me and to empower me to flee from sin so I may overcome. Lord, I pray your Word: "Trust in the LORD with all your heart, and lean not on your own understanding; in all your ways acknowledge Him, and He shall direct your paths."*

*Father, help me by Your Spirit to do that. I look to You, the source of my help. And I know that You are willing and able to keep me from falling, and to present me faultless before the presence of Your glory with exceeding joy. To my only wise God and my Savior, be glory and majesty, dominion and power, both now and ever. I love You, Lord. Amen.*

And behold, I am coming quickly, and My reward is with Me, to give to every one according to his work. I am the Alpha and the Omega, the Beginning and the End, the First and the Last. *Blessed are those who do His commandments, that they may have the right to the tree of life, and may enter through the gates into the city.* But outside are dogs and sorcerers and sexually immoral and murderers and idolaters, and *whoever loves and practices a lie.* I, Jesus, have sent My angel to testify to you these things in the churches. I am the Root and the Offspring of David, the Bright and Morning Star. And the Spirit and the bride say, "Come!" And let him who hears say, "Come!" And let him who thirsts come. Whoever desires, let him take the water of life freely.

-REVELATION 22:12-17, EMPHASIS ADDED

## Godliness for gain

Some follow Jesus not because they love Him for who He is, but only for what they can get from Him. Unless they truly repent, this wrong motive, poor character, and selfish desire eclipses their love for God Himself, and it can have eternal consequences.

Remember Judas Iscariot. In the ministry with Jesus as one of His twelve chosen disciples, he illustrates this principle well.

1.　List some ways in which Judas is an example of this truth.

_____

_____

_____

_____

_____

## Lifestyles

Some teach that you can live a completely worldly, sinful life and yet be saved because you once prayed a prayer. Others teach that you must obtain salvation through your good works and self-controlled life. Neither is accurate nor biblical.

Therefore by their fruits you will know them. Not everyone who says to Me, "Lord, Lord," shall enter the kingdom of heaven, but he who does the will of My Father in heaven. Many will say to Me in that day, "Lord, Lord, have we not prophesied in Your name, cast out demons in Your name, and done many wonders in Your name?" And then I will declare to them, "I never knew you; depart from Me, you who practice lawlessness!"

-MATTHEW 7:20-23

2. What is the important contrast Matthew 7 is showing us?

_____

_____

_____

_____

_____

Jesus is not preaching salvation only by good works. Rather He is saying that when you receive Him as Lord, His nature is imparted into you and He gives you the ability to obey God. Each day you have choices about whether you will follow Him or not. In this passage the original Greek word for "lawlessness" is *anomia*, which means acting contrary to the law or to the will of God.

## Turning away

Jesus freely offers eternal life. His spirit draws us to Himself and we can be saved. His nature and His grace within us empowers us to walk in His ways and to please Him. With salvation He allows us the freedom to choose to follow Him as loving disciples or even to depart from the faith.

But you don't just "lose" your salvation like you lose a pen or pencil or misplace your car keys or wallet.

Ezekiel speaks of purposely, willfully, turning away from righteousness and doing abominations that the wicked man does:

> But when a righteous man turns away from his righteousness and commits iniquity, and does according to all the abominations that the wicked man does, shall he live? All the righteousness which he has done shall not be remembered; because of the unfaithfulness of which he is guilty and the sin which he has committed, because of them he shall die.
>
> -EZEKIEL 18:24

3. In our mistakes, what is the evidence we have not permanently walked away from the faith?

_____

_____

_____

_____

_____

This subject causes a healthy fear of the Lord (Prov. 9:10). It is also very counter to today's culture. We live in a society that for the most part believes there is no such thing as absolute truth. Yet the Bible teaches the exact opposite. *Scriptures clearly teach that true faith in Christ results in repentance of sin and a life of obedience to Christ.*

4.  What are some ways this is counter to today's popular lifestyles?

    _____
    _____
    _____
    _____

---

**hot TOPIC** — This may be a new subject or concept for you. Write down what you are thinking and feeling about the following statement: "Jesus said He would not lose any the Father gives Him (John 18:9), because He would never leave us or forsake us. But He didn't say that we couldn't leave Him."

_____
_____
_____
_____
_____

There will be Christians who at one time truly followed Jesus but eventually turned from His ways, permanently bringing forth their fatal end. God gives believers the desire and the power to follow Him, but He does not make robots of us. He lets us freely decide whether or not we will indeed love and follow Him.

---

## The Scriptures Speak

For if, after they have escaped the pollutions of the world through the knowledge of the Lord and Savior Jesus Christ, they are again entangled in them and overcome, the latter end is worse for them than the beginning. For it would have been better for them not to have known the way of righteousness, than having known it, to turn from the holy commandment delivered to them. But it has happened to them according to the true proverb: "A dog returns to his own vomit," and, "a sow, having washed, to her wallowing in the mire."

-2 PETER 2:20-22

5.  Why would it be better to never have known Jesus, then to have known Him and permanently walk away?

    _____
    _____
    _____
    _____
    _____

*These are spots in your love feasts, while they feast with you without fear, serving only themselves. They are clouds without water, carried about by the winds; late autumn trees without fruit, twice dead, pulled up by the roots; raging waves of the sea, foaming up their own shame; wandering stars for whom is reserved the blackness of darkness forever.*

-Jude 12-13

6. How does this happen to someone?

7. What is the end result?

The writer of Hebrews tells us that it is impossible for a person who chooses to permanently walk away from Christ to be restored.

For it is impossible for those who were once enlightened, and have tasted of the heavenly gift, and were made partakers of the Holy Ghost, and have tasted the good word of God, and the powers of the world to come, if they shall fall away, to renew them again unto repentance; seeing they crucify to themselves the Son of God afresh, and put him to an open shame.

-HEBREWS 6:4-6, KJV

## Rejoice! God is Able to Keep You from Stumbling

*We should not serve God to earn His approval; we should serve God because we are in love with Him!*

- JOHN BEVERE

The following verses are full of strength, hope, and encouragement:

And everyone who has this hope in Him purifies himself, just as He is pure.

-1 JOHN 3:3

But ye, beloved, building up yourselves on your most holy faith, praying in the Holy Ghost, keep yourselves in the love of God, looking for the mercy of our Lord Jesus Christ unto eternal life.

-JUDE 20-21, KJV

He will keep you strong to the end, so that you will be blameless on the day of our Lord Jesus Christ.

-1 CORINTHIANS 1:8, NIV

Now unto him that is able to keep you from falling, and to present you faultless before the presence of his glory with exceeding joy, to the only wise God our Saviour, be glory and majesty, dominion and power, both now and ever. Amen.

-JUDE 24-25, KJV

8. What do those verses mean to you personally now that you have completed this hour's session?

_____

_____

_____

_____

**ZENITH**
the time when
something is
most powerful
or successful.

There are many important Scriptures in this session, certainly worthy of more study. Which one will have the most lasting impact on you? Why?

_____

_____

_____

_____

_____

_____

_____

_____

_____

_____

_____

_____

_____

_____

_____

_____

# HOUR 5

Please refer to Chapter 7,

The Foundation,

in the *Driven by Eternity* book

and video session 5.

**Week 5 · Day 1**

*All my possessions*
*for a moment*
*in time.*

-LAST WORDS OF
QUEEN ELIZABETH I

Although it is doubtful whether these actually were the last words of the queen, they have become a popular anecdote. Perhaps this is because they resonate with us. Nearly everyone seems to understand that "you can't take it with you." When you die, you die; you go to the grave one way or the other, and all the wealth, power, or influence in the world cannot gain you another precious moment or return you to previous wondrous moments.

Everyone knows death is elementary in the sense that it is a basic fundamental part of every person's life, without any exception. **We all know we will die. But there is another dimension to death as well.** For Christians, for believers in other religions, and for multitudes of people professing no religion at all, the sense that death brings with it some sort of judgment seems almost innate, possessed from birth.

The writer of Hebrews tells us that one of the foundational gospel truths is eternal judgment. This makes complete sense when viewed in light of what we have said here. It is a foundational truth because it is as basic, as real, and as certain as death itself. Death is the doorway to eternity through which we all will pass, and after that, judgment.

And as it is appointed for men to die once, but after this the judgment...

-HEBREWS 9:27

This is a foundational, imperative truth, and it must be part and parcel with all gospel teaching and with every Christian's lifestyle. It is as elementary to our faith as reading, writing, and arithmetic are to our earliest school lessons. And even more so, of course, for we are speaking of our eternal destiny.

So come on, let's leave the preschool fingerpainting exercises on Christ and get on with the grand work of art. Grow up in Christ. The basic foundational truths are in place: turning your back on "salvation by self-help" and turning in trust toward God; baptismal instructions; laying on of hands; resurrection of the dead; eternal judgment. God helping us, we'll stay true to all that.

-HEBREWS 6:1-3, THE MESSAGE

Let's focus on the essentials, building on a sure foundation so that when the winds blow, we will stand and not fall. So when we die, we may live indeed.

Living with the proper understanding of eternal judgment in mind is essential. How does this integrate with your daily life?

_____

_____

_____

_____

## Week 5 · Day 2

*"Newsweek" just did a survey. Sixty-nine percent of the evangelical Christians – not Protestant – but evangelical – believe that you can get saved other than through Jesus. Sixty-nine percent. I saw it with my own eyes – I bought two of them because I was like, you're kidding me!*

-JOHN BEVERE,
IN ASTONISHMENT

Of course a loving God is attractive to masses of people. Who wouldn't want to be a part of the "in" group that is growing and has many freedoms, some influence, much prosperity, and a wealth of knowledge? Certainly there is a lot that can be attained through putting into practice some basic principles that can easily be pulled from the Bible.

In many of today's Christian theological systems – though they are not yet well documented systematically – there exists such an entangling with non-Christian teachings that it is hard to tell where one begins and the other ends. Interweaving God's Holy Word with pop culture as well as ancient philosophies can be a tremendous way to attract adherents and increase numbers.

In many ways that principle can be fine, of course. Why throw the baby out with the proverbial bathwater? There is much contemporary data and volumes of ancient material that are helpful, biblical, and relevant. But we must be ever vigilant, always diligent (two very unpopular concepts in today's society, unfortunately) to be certain the contemporary and ancient ideas that are brought together with Scripture are consistent with biblical truth. This means work, it takes time, and it demands commitment, but we are empowered.

Unless we are firmly established in biblical truth, we are ever prevented from building a proper and healthy life in Christ. This definitely – according to Scripture itself – includes the basics of the love and goodness as well as the fear and sovereignty of God. And if after we die – which we must – we are judged (which we will be), then we'd best take heed to the many biblical admonishments to intimately know God, to study, to meditate in the Word, to pray, to follow God's precepts, etc.

Why chance your eternal destiny to anything other than biblical truth?

When He had called the people to Himself, with His disciples also, He said to them, "Whoever desires to come after Me, let him deny himself, and take up his cross, and follow Me."

-MARK 8:34

What is the Lord saying to you about searching the Scriptures, following Christ, and ensuring you're on the right path to eternity?

_____

_____

_____

_____

_____

## Week 5 · Day 3

*I tell you, my friends...I will show you whom you should fear. Fear him who, after the killing of the body, has power to throw you into hell. Yes, I tell you, fear him.*

-JESUS CHRIST,
IN LUKE 12:4-5, NIV

Some would say all fear is bad. But that is a foolish generalization. Some fear is bad, but some is healthy and saves us. Fear of being run over keeps us from playing in front of speeding cars. Fear of fire keeps us from burning ourselves. Fear of drowning causes us to learn to swim and have good sense when doing it. There are wonderful Bible verses that say: "There is no fear in love; but perfect love casts out fear" (1 John 4:18); "God is love" (1 John 4:8); and, "For God has not given us a spirit of fear, but of power and of love and of a sound mind" (2 Tim. 1:7).

To fear God is to reverence Him, esteem Him, and honor Him – not to be afraid of Him.

> Therefore, since we are receiving a kingdom which cannot be shaken, let us have grace, by which we may serve God acceptably with reverence and godly fear.
>
> -HEBREWS 12:28

God is greatly to be feared in the assembly of the saints, and to be held in reverence by all those around Him.

-PSALM 89:7

In fact, it is the unbeliever who doesn't fear God. Hear King David, who was called a man after God's own heart:

An oracle within my heart concerning the transgression of the wicked: There is no fear of God before his eyes.

-PSALM 36:1

When the unbeliever gets a glimpse of the realities of God, he is stricken with fear. God is too wonderful and awesome to behold, other than by His grace and mercy. Those who lose the fear of God tend to think He doesn't see them in all they do. The books of Ezekiel, Jeremiah, and Isaiah contain examples of people who began to say, "The Lord doesn't see," thus reducing Him to their level and allowing them to do as they please.

But when you have the true fear of God, you know there's nothing secret that won't be known. Nothing hidden that won't be brought to the light at the judgment. So you live your life a totally different way. It's a solid foundation. *If we lack the fear of God, we can be deceived that things are overlooked and take comfort in an unscriptural mercy that does not exist.*

How have you understood the fear of the Lord up to this point? Has your view changed?

# Week 5 · Day 4

*Attaining and maintaining a good understanding of eternal judgment and punishment firmly plants the fear of the Lord in our hearts.*

-JOHN BEVERE

Eternal judgment is a foundational biblical truth (Heb. 6:1-3). The fear of God is also to be a basic element in the believer's life. This godly fear can be a river from which springs obedience.

But is God angry at us? Is He always looking to give us a good beating, frustrate and taunt us, then finally relish in it as He sends us to hell? Does He want us scared of Him? Hardly. Jesus came in love, by love, and for love.

Yet godly fear is a very real part of love. Any child who has ever been loved by a good parent, aunt, grandpa, or guardian knows a part of that love was genuine fear – good, healthy fear. Not being scared of them, but holding them in reverence, understanding their position and authority, and appreciating it. When you know they have the power to hug you and hold you as well as judge you and sentence you – whether that earns "time out" on a chair or being "grounded" when you foul up – you know you need to respect them. And deep down you know that fear keeps you safe, healthy, and on the straight and narrow. You are ultimately glad they cared enough about you to have loved you and taught you in the right way.

Moses said to the people, "Do not be afraid. God has come to test you, so that the fear of God will be with you to keep you from sinning."

-EXODUS 20:20, NIV

Do you see it? "Fear not," Moses says, and then in the same breath, "so that the fear of God will be with you." Well, which is it? Fear not...or be afraid? Old or New Testament, the principle is the same. Don't be afraid or scared of God. God's desire is to be intimate with you. How can you be intimate with someone you are afraid of? Intimacy is the key. When you are intimate with someone, you don't want to hurt them. The fear of God will keep you from sinning, directing and guiding your ways, which will in turn decide your destiny.

The test is, do you approach Him and continue to hold Him in the reverence due Him? When we do this, we keep ourselves protected, safe, and healthy. You see, God is the best, loving, kind, wonderful daddy in the universe. *But He is also the "King" who is almighty and just.*

Have you experienced God as daddy *and* King in your personal time with Him? Explain.

_____

_____

_____

_____

# Week 5 · Day 5

*The definition of the fear of the Lord is to honor Him. It is to esteem Him above anything or anyone else. It is to value, respect, and reverence Him above anything or anyone else. So, therefore, what He loves, you love. What He hates, you hate. What is important to Him is important to you. What is not so important to Him isn't so important to you.*

-JOHN BEVERE

Certainly among the millions who call themselves Christians today the tendency in faith and lifestyle is more toward liberality, even biblical lawlessness, than to the opposite, which is legalism. Contemporary society is by and large running to and fro when it comes to Judeo-Christian values and behavior. In the early church there were those same types of challenges, but the bigger threat of the two was legalism. Trying to attain faith and salvation by keeping the law was a serious problem. Today that is eclipsed by the opposite end of the spectrum. The law and its associated values are being trodden underfoot, even in the church.

Marriage, the definition of family, sexuality, the sanctity of life, and even the most basic ideas of truth, honor, integrity, and fidelity are being redefined according to a self-styled philosophy. People are asking what truth is and then making it up as they go along to suit selfish needs.

It will take the love and fear of God to change our nation. Both bring us to God and keep us healthy and in the middle of the straight and narrow road to eternal life, not in the ditch on either side. **If all you have is fear, you're a legalist. If you only have love, you tend to become lawless.**

Do not be haughty, but fear. For if God did not spare the natural branches, He may not spare you either. Therefore consider the goodness and severity of God: on those who fell, severity; but toward you, goodness, if you continue in His goodness. Otherwise you also will be cut off.

-ROMANS 11:20-22

Is your life balanced with the fear of the Lord, or are you living to one of the two extremes? How can you become more balanced in your walk with the Lord?

_____

_____

_____

_____

_____

_____

## Week 5 · Day 6

*We have not been an eternally driven church in America in these last several years. What we've done is built churches that are large. In order to keep them growing we've shied away from preaching the whole counsel of God.*

-JOHN BEVERE

The Barna Group recently conducted a study showing a huge gap between how church leaders saw the spirituality of their congregations versus the reality of people's devotion to God. One out of every seven adults (15 percent), and more specifically, among those who attend Protestant churches, not quite one out of every four (23 percent), named their faith in God as their top priority in life.[1]

It should surprise no one that nonbelievers wouldn't list faith in God at the top of their list of priorities. But that anyone who calls himself a Christian would not is a real eye-opener. If devotion to God is not a believer's top priority, then what is? It can be discussed endlessly what that devotion must look like *but shouldn't it be a given that followers of Christ would make their top priority following Christ?*

From intimacy with God all things flow. Jesus the Savior, the Lord, 100 percent God, 100 percent man, sinless, perfectly obedient, put it this way:

Anyone who drinks the water I give will never thirst – not ever. The water I give will be an artesian spring within, gushing fountains of endless life.
-JOHN 4:14, THE MESSAGE

The believer who commits to putting relationship with God first will have a wellspring of divine life within. Supernatural, this endless living and dynamic resource provides everything needed to face and overcome in life. Further, this wellspring of life provides the resources necessary to reach out and overflow upon multitudes of others. The carrier of this powerful fountain of vitality can influence everyone with whom he or she comes into contact.

But first things first. Devotion to Christ means exactly that. He will take no second row, no backseat, no number two ranking on our "to-do" list of life. Why would anyone want to do that anyway, when He offers so much? Yes, you will have to lose your way of life to gain His, but is there a substitute for peace, godliness with contentment, love, and ultimately heaven? Even more, what about His character? When you die to yourself and seek His face and His ways, you will become more like Him. You will develop His character. How exciting to be more like the King of the universe!

God is a jealous God in the best of ways. He wants us for Himself and will settle for nothing less than a bride that gives herself willingly and with desire to His incomparable ways of love.

If you find it difficult to put Him first in your life, He has provided Himself as the answer.

For God is at work within you, helping you want to obey him, and then helping you do what he wants.

-PHILIPPIANS 2:13, TLB

*Could it be more attractive than that? He gives you the "want to."* Do you lack desire for Him and His ways? *Just ask the giver of desire.* Journal your prayer, asking God to help you want to obey Him, talking in sweet intimacy with the One who loves you as no one else can.

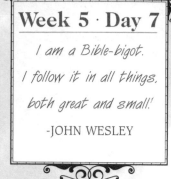

*I am a Bible-bigot.*
*I follow it in all things,*
*both great and small!*

-JOHN WESLEY

What we follow determines where we will end up. If you want to get to heaven, you need to follow the maker of heaven.

> You laid earth's foundations a long time ago,
> and handcrafted the very heavens.
> -PSALM 102:25, THE MESSAGE

Daily life's path to eternal glory is the road walked by Jesus Christ. We follow Him, in His ways, by His Spirit's empowerment. The final steps of life are the passage called death. In death we come face to face with eternity. "Forever" is a long time.

We might use a popular sports term to describe it at that point and say, "Game over!" Win or lose, you're done. No more periods of play, no more attempts or valiant efforts, training or preparation, or chances to score and win, no more rulings by officials. Everything is complete in glorious or horrid finality.

We may just as easily use the other sports saying though: "Game on!" Because when you cross over by that final exit, you have to give account of everything you've done, how you lived, and how you played the game.

> For we must all appear before the judgment seat of Christ, that each one may receive what is due to him for the things done while in the body, whether good or bad. Since, then, we know what it is to fear the Lord, we try to persuade men.
> -2 CORINTHIANS 5:10-11, NIV

Scary? For sure, if you are unprepared. Send a guy who hasn't put on a uniform in years to play quarterback at the Super Bowl, and he'll get crushed. Maybe the talent and skills were there, maybe the heart is there, but with no preparation he'd be destroyed.

How do you prepare for eternity? George Whitefield was a famous contemporary of John Wesley, the famous founder of the Methodist Church. The great revivalist preacher Whitefield was once asked why he always preached on John 3:7: "Do not marvel that I said to you, 'You must be born again.'" Whitefield's reply? "Because...you must be born again!"[2]

And so it still is today. You must be born again by the Spirit of God, and you must indeed follow the Lord in His ways, loving what He loves and hating what He hates. If you are saved and bearing the fruit of salvation, you are prepared for eternity.

*Driven by Eternity:*
## YOUR WEEK IN REVIEW

- Time is precious.

- We must be firmly established in biblical truth

- To be a Christian, a believer, means to fear God.

- Eternal judgment is a foundational biblical truth (Heb. 6:1-3).

- Godly fear is a river from which springs obedience.

- The balance between fear and love keeps us on the straight and narrow.

- If we say we are a Christian, we will see the evidence that Christ is the priority in our life.

Take a bit of time and think on this exquisite truth: God is a jealous God in the best of ways. He wants us for Himself and will settle for nothing less than a bride that gives herself willingly and with desire to His incomparable ways of love.

Give yourself to Him. Pray in your own words, letting the Lord minister to you as you minister to Him. Journal the miracle of His time with you today.

1. *The Journal of the Rev. John Wesley*, A.M. (London: Charles H. Kelly, 1911), V: 169, June 5, 1766 entry.
2. Colin C. Whittaker, *Great Revivals* (Springfield, MO: Gospel Publishing House, n.d.), 51.

**YOUR ETERNAL DESTINY:** You can join the men and women who walk in the fear of the Lord, changing history one life at a time! The setting is Great Britain, in the 1730s:

> "The whole population seemed to be given over to an orgy of drunkenness which made the very name of Englishmen to stink in the nostrils of other nations," says Silvester Horne in his *Popular History of The Free Churches*....A common sign outside the pubs was "Drunk for a penny. Dead drunk for two. Straw to lie on"...The theatre was shockingly vulgar and depraved. (John) Wesley referred to it as "the obscenity of the stage – that stink of all corruption." The literature of the period would even today be classed mostly as hard core pornography. Polygamy, fornication, homosexuality, were not considered sinful. Violence was rampant. Gangs of drunken ruffians paraded the streets and subjected women to nameless outrages and defenseless men to abominable tortures. The constables shared the drunken habits of the time and were mainly corrupt....And what was the church doing before 1739? For the most part, sleeping. Bishop Ryle wrote, "Both parties [Anglicans and Non-conformists] seemed at least agreed on one point – and that was to let the devil alone and do nothing for hearts and souls."[1]

And we think we have it tough today! Onto that desperate scene stepped a thirty-five-year-old John Wesley. Middle aged, five foot five inches tall, 126 pounds, this holiness preacher would eventually command the attention of multitudes.

### Brilliant scholar

A brilliant Oxford scholar, ordained a deacon in the Church of England in 1725, elected a fellow of Lincoln College, Oxford, in 1726, ordained as a minister in the Church of England in 1728, and a man of organizational genius, Wesley loved good friends, tennis, riding, and swimming. However, because he knew there was something missing from his religion, at Oxford he formed a group of students that included his younger brother, Charles Wesley, and George Whitefield (each of whom would go on to international honor and acclaim in their own right to this very day). They were derisively called "Methodists" for their methodical devotion to religious duties.

### Failed missionary

Failing as a missionary to the colonies in America, including an unfortunate love affair with a woman that ended up in court, Wesley returned to England. But the two-year mission wasn't a total loss. During the long transatlantic voyage to the colonies, several great storms threatened to destroy the ship. He had been impressed with a group of Moravians who showed no fear, but rather calm confidence and faith in God during the storms. On the way back he recalled this and wrote, "I went to America to convert the Indians; but oh! who shall convert me?"[2]

## An encounter with God

Back in London, on Wednesday, May 24, 1738, Wesley went to a meeting on Aldersgate Street. As a result of the sermon, Wesley wrote, "About a quarter before nine, while he was describing the changes which God works in the heart through faith in Christ, I felt my heart strangely warmed. I felt I did trust in Christ, Christ alone for salvation; and an assurance was given me that he had taken away my sins, even mine, and saved me from the law of sin and death."[3] From that point on he was a changed man. Gone was his reliance on rules and works for salvation. Joy replaced striving. Now his emphasis was on faith in the risen Savior alone, and good works would flow from a heart and life filled with the constant presence of the Holy Spirit.

## A changed man

Wesley started revivals in England that shook the nation and brought reform and revival to other nations as well. The founder of Methodism, his impact on the world is immeasurable. Besides preaching and writing, he and his Methodists always reached out and worked among the poor and hurting, the neglected and needy. He pioneered innovative methods and preached to large gatherings of thousands in the open air in a time with no microphones. Often people would cry out in agony as they came under conviction of the Holy Spirit. They would drown out his preaching and often fall on the ground under God's power.

In contrast, in October 1743 a mob enraged by the gospel yelled, "Kill him," "Crucify him," and a violent blow made his mouth and nose gush with blood. Yet in the end he was rescued by the very man who had led the mob![4]

Wesley and the Methodists were attacked and persecuted by other clergymen and leaders in sermons and in print. They were denounced as having strange doctrines and causing religious disturbances. Called fanatics, they were accused of leading people astray, claiming miraculous gifts, and of attacking other clergy and the established church.

Seeming as one wholly possessed by God, Wesley lived as a man from another world. He rose at four in the morning, lived simply and methodically, and was almost never idle. Though substantial funds came to his ministry, he used little for himself, and he died poor. Wesley's message served as a basis for the Holiness movement, from which came Pentecostalism, much of the Charismatic movement, and the Christian and Missionary Alliance. His challenge for personal holiness and social involvement is still at work in the church today.

Going into eternity to be with the Lord at eighty-eight years of age, he had traveled 250,000 miles on horseback, preached 45,000 sermons, wrote 233 books or pamphlets, and helped with the writing of more than 100 others. His titanic achievements for God have seldom been equaled.[5] He left behind 140,000 Methodist members (including churches and leaders still revered today), fifteen years of journaling, and 1,500 traveling preachers![6]

What do you see in the story of John Wesley *for you*? Remember, he was far from perfect. He began on the wrong foot believing and stressing works, not intimacy with God. As an unsuccessful missionary he was in a love affair that took him into court. He probably wasn't truly converted until well into his career, he had a difficult marriage, and he didn't begin to have success in ministry until he was thirty-five. God works mightily in and through each of us if we just will earnestly seek Him as Wesley did.

1. What is God saying to *you*?

_____

_____

_____

_____

_____

## Answers from another world!

Nowadays, the earth and its more than six billion people seem in such a state that it might appear hopeless to turn it from its momentum of sin and worldliness. *Other-worldliness* is what we need. The same Spirit that blessed Wesley lives in God's people today, and our world is not much more or less difficult to reach than his was.

> *To follow Jesus means you become an alien. You become a citizen of another country, a country that doesn't jive and correspond with any society that's here on this earth. You will be constantly going against the grain of any culture on this earth if you are truly going to live as a kingdom person.*
>
> -JOHN BEVERE

Many people want to believe in UFOs (unidentified flying objects), alien species, and peoples or beings from other planets. Indeed, this may be an attempt to fill the deep desire many have for a belief in something beyond themselves, something greater than the earth, bigger, better, more fantastic than the day-to-day mundane life they live and see all around them. Certainly the incredible expanse of galaxy upon galaxy that science tries to make known to us is very telling. There is something bigger, there is much more to us than we know.

2. Why do you think people have a desire for or fantasize about things like this?

_____

_____

_____

_____

_____

3. What or whom do you think is the answer to the world's longings and challenges?

There may be nothing wrong with a good science-fiction story, but do we need to dream of alien encounters when the answer is already present among us? God has declared and sent His only begotten Son and given the Holy Spirit to live inside those who would be His children.

Yes, there is more to this life and the universe than meets the eye. And the real story *has been* declared by angels – the real heavenly beings – in Luke's Gospel, chapter two. And it was (historically) witnessed by hundreds (1 Cor. 15) and testified to by millions since. And the Messiah Himself testified to another kingdom:

And He said to them, "You are from beneath; I am from above. You are of this world; I am not of this world. Therefore I said to you that you will die in your sins; for if you do not believe that I am He, you will die in your sins."

-JOHN 8:23-24

Jesus answered, "My kingdom is not of this world. If My kingdom were of this world, My servants would fight, so that I should not be delivered to the Jews; but now My kingdom is not from here."

-JOHN 18:36

This is a faithful saying and worthy of all acceptance, that Christ Jesus came into the world to save sinners.

-1 TIMOTHY 1:15

When you wrote your answer above, you may have said Jesus was the answer, and of course you are correct. But...do you realize you are only partially correct? Look at these verses and answer the question again.

You are the light of the world. A city that is set on a hill cannot be hidden.

-MATTHEW 5:14

But sanctify the Lord God in your hearts, and always be ready to give a defense to everyone who asks you a reason for the hope that is in you, with meekness and fear.

-1 PETER 3:15

But you shall receive power when the Holy Spirit has come upon you; and you shall be witnesses to Me in Jerusalem, and in all Judea and Samaria, and to the end of the earth.

-ACTS 1:8

As Jesus was getting into the boat, the man who had been demon-possessed begged to go with him. Jesus did not let him, but said, "Go home to your family and tell them how much the Lord has done for you, and how he has had mercy on you."

-MARK 5:18-19, NIV

4. Based on these Scriptures, now who do you think is the answer to the world's longings and challenges?

_____

_____

_____

_____

_____

If we are to have an impact on the earth, we must believe and live out Christ-like character. When speaking of great women and men of faith, the writer of Hebrews says:

These all died in faith, not having received the promises, but having seen them afar off were assured of them, embraced them and *confessed that they were strangers and pilgrims on the earth.* For those who say such things declare plainly that they seek a homeland. And truly if they had called to mind that country from which they had come out, they would have had opportunity to return. *But now they desire a better, that is, a heavenly country. Therefore God is not ashamed to be called their God, for He has prepared a city for them.*

-HEBREWS 11:13-16, EMPHASIS ADDED

If we are tied to the world and its ways, we cannot hope to offer God's answers. From Genesis to Revelation we see that people who blessed their neighbors, who made a difference to towns or cities, or even changed nations were those who lived as strangers and pilgrims on the earth and walked in intimate love with God in the fear of God and the power of His Spirit.

5. Do you "desire a better, heavenly country" like Abraham, David, Rahab, Joseph, Peter, Paul, and others? In what ways does your life prove you are a stranger, a pilgrim on the earth?

_____

_____

_____

_____

_____

## Holy Fear: A Solid Foundation

Therefore, leaving the discussion of the elementary principles of Christ, let us go on to perfection, not laying again the foundation of repentance from dead works and of faith toward God, of the doctrine of baptisms, of laying on of hands, of resurrection of the dead, and of eternal judgment.

-HEBREWS 6:1-2

6. Why is eternal judgment a foundational principle of Christ?

_____
_____
_____
_____
_____

7. What does the fear of the Lord have to do with eternal judgment and punishment?

_____
_____
_____
_____
_____

8. What is fueled by fear of the Lord?

_____
_____
_____
_____
_____

Deuteronomy 5:29 says, "Oh, that they had such a heart in them that they would fear Me and always keep all My commandments, that it might be well with them and with their children forever!"

9. What are the five manifestations of the fear of God?

1. _____

2. _____

3. _____

4. _____

5. _____

10. How does the fear of the Lord give us confidence at the judgment?

_____

_____

_____

_____

_____

11. What is it that all will be tested in, as Adam, Eve, and even Lucifer were? And what does it mean to you at the judgment?

_____

_____

_____

_____

_____

12. By all modern accounts, Jesus loses a convert when He speaks with the rich young ruler in Mark 10. Yet why is it said that Jesus loved him?

_____

_____

_____

_____

_____

---

**hot TOPIC**   Are you walking in the fear, obedience and power of the Lord? How can that make YOU a world-influencer?

_____

_____

_____

_____

_____

_____

_____

_____

_____

_____

_____

**ZENITH**
the time when
something is
most powerful
or successful.

Not everyone is called to be a John Wesley. What has God called *you* to do as His influencer today?

_____

_____

1. Colin C. Whittaker, *Great Revivals* (Springfield, MO: Gospel Publishing House, n.d.), 50.
2. Keith J. Hardman, *The Spiritual Awakeners* (Wheaton, IL: Moody Press, n.d.), 94.
3. Ibid.
4. Whittaker, *Great Revivals*, 60.
5. Hardman, *The Spiritual Awakeners*, 93.
6. Whittaker, *Great Revivals*, 61.

# THE DAY OF JUDGMENT 2

Five hundred Endelites are gathered in the
Hall of Life, anxiously awaiting their
first meeting with King Jalyn.
Suddenly the Royal Guards enter the hall.
All activity comes to a halt as the
Chief Guard addresses the group.
*"Shortly you will face your king,"*
he declares. Who will be first?

PLEASE REFER TO CHAPTER 8 IN THE
*Driven by Eternity* BOOK OR THE *Affabel* CD SET

# SELFISH IS JUDGED

Selfish is the first person called to this judgment. He immediately thinks this is a good thing, because he was mayor of Endel, an important figure. But if Selfish had been thinking rightly, in terms of Scripture, he would have thought differently.

Selfish remembered the ancient writings that told of great rewards for those who ruled well, but he didn't seem to remember other verses. In fact, he felt certain he would be given a throne! We tend to have selective memory when we go about our own ways in life, but the judgments we see in Affabel challenge us to live according to all the Scripture, not just the verses that fit our imaginations, our personal agendas, or selfish needs or goals.

> "For I say, through the grace given to me, to everyone who is among you, not to think of himself more highly than he ought to think, but to think soberly, as God has dealt to each one a measure of faith."
>
> -Romans 12:3

1. The Bible is full of simple instructions and warnings on how we should conduct our lives each day. Selfish could have been great in the kingdom had he but heeded the Word. The same goes for you in God's kingdom. How does Romans 12:3 apply to Selfish (and to you)?

## Social, an old friend

2. On the way to meet Jalyn, Selfish meets Social, whose name has been changed to Content. What are the implications of this name change? Why from Social to Content?

3. Selfish learns that Social doesn't have a great position in Affabel, and Selfish is shocked because of how great Social had been in Endel. By what standard is Selfish judging the life and actions of Social?

4. What was it Social wished he had done, so he would have received a greater reward?

**5** Why didn't he do it? What was the reason Social lived the way he did, with the result that he didn't receive a greater reward?

## The Word: blessing or curse

There is something special and of the utmost importance in how Jalyn and those in Affabel speak. Jalyn always *answers with simple straightforward verses of Scripture just as Christ will do with us at the Judgment Seat. The Word of God says we will be judged by what He has already spoken.*

This seems a curse to those who didn't follow His ways, because it gives no room for excuses or to hide. But it is a blessing to the obedient.

When Selfish met Social and others, they all had regrets about how they didn't heed many Scriptures they had known of. Social at one point tells Selfish:

*"You knew this from the ancient writings taught in class. Though I doubt you would have acknowledged you believed them while in Endel."*

The Scriptures speak loudly and clearly of the basics of how we are to live now in this life. *Yet though we know, we often bury these truths, allowing them (for many reasons) to lie dormant within us.*

**6** Why do we do this?

DRIVEN BY ETERNITY GIVES YOU AN UNPRECEDENTED OPPORTUNITY, A SORT OF "VIRTUAL JUDGMENT" TO PREPARE YOU FOR ETERNITY!

GOD HAS PROVIDED THIS AMAZING GLIMPSE INTO THE REALITIES OF THE JUDGMENT SO YOU CAN BE READY TO MEET YOUR KING, JESUS!

**Avoid the snares and traps that cause you to live a life that you will regret. Make right choices now for a life that puts God's Word and His ways first.**
In many ways this Scripture sums up this message:

For if we would judge ourselves, we would not be judged.

-1 Corinthians 11:31

**7** How and with what are we to judge ourselves?

8   What does 1 Corinthians 11:31 mean to you in your real-life situations right now?

9   What could it mean to your eternity?

### Fame or folly?

On his way to meet Jalyn, Selfish also met Motivator, who was his favorite teacher in Endel. Motivator shocks Selfish when he speaks with him, summing things up with this statement: *"The foundation the ancient apostle spoke of is the lordship of Jalyn, which we both know is the only way a person can enter this kingdom. However, once we truly belong to him, we should build upon this foundation. When measured by the ancient writings, my life fell short...I lost my reward."*

Use your own words and 1 Corinthians 3:12-15 to describe why this famous teacher received one of the lowest positions in Affabel.

> Now if anyone builds on this foundation with gold, silver, precious stones, wood, hay, straw, each one's work will become clear; for the Day will declare it, because it will be revealed by fire; and the fire will test each one's work, of what sort it is. If anyone's work which he has built on it endures, he will receive a reward. If anyone's work is burned, he will suffer loss; but he himself will be saved, yet so as through fire.
>
> -1 Corinthians 3:12-15

10   Consider if your name would be changed at the judgment seat. How do you feel about this?

11   What was the important difference between Endel and Affabel, which became a trap for Motivator's life and part of the reason he lived the way he did?

12   Is there anything now that is trapping you that is not based on Kingdom principles?

*13* Patient's humble lifestyle and seemingly insignificant acts of service to her King had huge impact. What were some of the simple yet profound things Patient had done in her life that led to such great eternal value?

At the judgment it is too late for change or repentance. Your life has already been lived, and the sentence will be eternal, with no chance for appeal or argument.

After seeing his life in review, before any sentence is pronounced, Selfish cries out, *"I deserve to be punished the rest of my life. I deserve Lone; I've wasted so much and produced so little in return for the talents and responsibilities I had."*

*14* What is the critical difference between how Selfish responded versus how Deceived, Double Life, Faint Heart, and Independent, who were sent to Lone, responded?

God is blessing you with the opportunity to live a life that can be richly rewarded! In life on earth, you too are approaching your great meeting with your King Jesus!

*15* Ask yourself the same types of questions that Selfish finds himself asking as he approaches His King:

- What are your true motives in life?
- What are your deepest intentions?
- Do you serve for your King's glory or out of selfish ambition?
- How have you conducted your life? Is it in line with the words of the King, or are you deceived as many others have been?
- Do you build up others, or do you use them to build your own success?
- What and how do you speak? *"But I say to you that for every idle word men may speak, they will give account of it in the day of judgment. For by your words you will be justified, and by your words you will be condemned"* (Matt. 12:36-37).

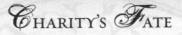

# CHARITY'S FATE

"But many who are first will be last; and the last first."

-Matthew 19:30

Charity is the last to be taken to see Jalyn. Yet this doesn't seem to concern her at all. As the guard comes for her and she begins her walk through the crowd in the Great Hall, you see many hints of the godly qualities she possesses.

*16.* Write down some of these godly qualities along with the hints that are given to reveal them.

It is not about power, fame, fortune, or influence. Remember Patient, who had been an unassuming secretary, little known, hardly recognized. Yet she received a great reward from Jalyn and a position as a ruler in Affabel! Charity was a small business owner. Although her business was successful, she was never included in the socials at the home of the mayor, Selfish. She wasn't asked to participate in leadership roles in the community. In fact, she was often excluded from things because of her simple obedient lifestyle. But she hardly seemed to notice. She was focused on reaching the less fortunate. She loved the weekly gatherings at the school and was always offering to help by giving or through serving in various roles.

**Get started and let it flow.**

Then the King will say to those on His right hand, "Come, you blessed of My Father, inherit the kingdom prepared for you from the foundation of the world: for I was hungry and you gave Me food; I was thirsty and you gave Me drink; I was a stranger and you took Me in; I was naked and you clothed Me; I was sick and you visited Me; I was in prison and you came to Me."

Then the righteous will answer Him, saying, "Lord, when did we see You hungry and feed You, or thirsty and give You drink? When did we see You a stranger and take You in, or naked and clothe You? Or when did we see You sick, or in prison, and come to You?" And the King will answer and say to them, "Assuredly, I say to you, inasmuch as you did it to one of the least of these My brethren, you did it to Me."

-Matthew 25:34-40

Charity was hardly even consciously aware of the many "little" things she was obedient in. She had simply followed closely the manner of life taught from the ancient writings. She lived according to the teachings and nature of her King and had as a result naturally lived for His heart.

Fulfilling Matthew 25 does not have to be intimidating or a big deal. We are all daily surrounded with plenty of needs, plenty of opportunities to be obedient to the Lord. He equips each of us if we will pray and take a few steps to serve Him and others! If you don't know where to start, then look and find somewhere.

*Take baby steps to follow the teachings of Jesus, and you will be amazed at how God strengthens both you and others through you! The more you obey, the more you will tend to obey and be blessed!*

17  What does Matthew 25:34-40 mean to you in your life right now?

18  How are you living it?

19  How might the Holy Spirit be leading you to be more obedient to the heart of God as seen in Matthew 25?

Often we live our lives awaiting the spectacular, the "big," the "important." Yet it is the daily living, the small things that God is watching, yearning for us to catch His vision and heart while we go about our business.

Let's look at Charity's life, the things she did, which resulted in great rewards for eternity.

- She gave to the school so others could be taught about Jalyn and His ways.
- She showed love to her fellow citizens through becoming involved in their lives.
- She refused to take part in careless or inappropriate activities and discussions.
- She was persecuted for her passion for Jalyn.
- She blessed others through her restaurant business, reaching out to wayward souls.
- She spent hours of sighing and weeping for the lost.
- She strictly adhered to Jalyn's ways, being excluded from socials because of her zeal for Jalyn.
- She refused to speak against fellow citizens or partake of gossip.
- And more…

God has certainly promised that He has given each of us, according to our abilities, all we need to joyfully serve Him and to be obedient to His Word! (See Matthew 25; Acts 11; Ephesians 4:16.)

## The gospel is...GREAT news!

There is nothing in Charity's list of accomplishments that is particularly outstanding or difficult. We all can give, we all can care, we all can refuse to take part in ungodly behavior, we all can pray and follow God's teachings in His Word! So what are you waiting for? This is GREAT news!

Be encouraged! God cares for you and desires to reward you! Take another look at Charity's list above. Listed are eight very straightforward ways in which she was an obedient, joyful servant.

How about you? Write down four simple everyday ways you too can live your life as one "driven by eternity" so you please God and are ready and eager to meet your King! Serving God is as simple as loving and following His ways, empowered by His Spirit. It is simple, yes, but it may not always be easy.

1.

2.

3.

4.

## The Keys

20 What one word was the key to Charity's great rewards?

Although we've noted that Charity's life was full of daily things we can all do, there is one thing which is remarkable: her *faithfulness* to actually live according to Jalyn's teachings. And we must have the same.

There were three reasons, three words, given by King Jalyn as to why Charity was welcomed to Affabel and made a great ruler and given a great mansion. Do you recall them?

## A great gift, a "trial run"!

"You therefore must endure hardship as a **good soldier** of Jesus Christ"
-2 Tim. 2:3, emphasis added

God often calls us soldiers in His spiritual army as we fight the good fight, which is a spiritual battle.

"Virtual combat" is when the armed forces engage in test exercises for combat skills without the use of live ammunition. And that is just how you may think of this message! You get a "dry-run"…a "get out of jail free card"…a chance to experience some of the realities of judgment day…**without the actual judgment so you can prepare for it!**

"Virtual reality" is a term that speaks of a world created by a computer, where you can enter and move around and interact with the things inside that world with no harm to yourself because it is not real. That is one of the best functions and purposes of this message. *Driven by Eternity* **can act as a trial exercise; a rehearsal and preparation for the most important moments in all of your life: death, judgment, and your eternal, never-ending destiny!**

## PRAYER AND CALL TO ACTION
### DON'T WASTE OR SQUANDER THIS GIFT, THIS OPPORTUNITY. WHAT ARE YOU GOING TO DO ABOUT THIS MESSAGE?

Father God, you have blessed me with this message so I can be ready to meet You. I pray right now and ask You to show me how You want me to respond, what You want me to do and the way You want me to live. As I write in this journal, Lord, I look to You to speak to me through Your Word and the Holy Spirit. Open my ears to hear, my eyes to see what The Spirit is saying to me. Help me empower me, by Your grace to live a life of obedience, no matter the circumstance, a life that is faithful, loyal, and humble, enduring to the end!

Thank You, Lord! I thank You and love You. I desire to serve You all the days of my life! Now to Him who is able to keep me unto that day…I commit myself in love, in Jesus' name, amen.

**21** **How is this series affecting your personal life?** One person described it "like going through a blender, at different speeds, with different ingredients, at once grinding, then smoothing, then chopping, then crunching…being molded and shaped"; others have wept and cried out to the Lord. Some have been greatly challenged in their thinking, living, or theology. Many have been changed and encouraged. Describe your experience.

**22** **Share together about the "virtual reality" aspect.** Has this seemed like a gift, a "trial run" to prepare for Judgment Day? How can you use it for this?

**23** **Are you realizing how God is judging YOU, alone?** There is no opportunity for you to point the finger at or be critical of others or shift blame.

**24** **What are you doing to be a light in the darkness, salt to the world?** Are you witnessing, sharing your faith, reaching out and doing the works of the gospel? Do you realize God has indeed equipped you?

Please refer to page 279 for info on ordering your *Affabel* CD Set

# HOUR

Please refer to Chapter 9,

Heaven,

in the *Driven by Eternity* book

and video session 6.

## Week 6 · Day 1

*Heaven is a very real place. It is not in the clouds with a bunch of spirits flying around with some kind of spiritual looking type of harps. It has buildings, it has trees, it has roads. And Paul himself was there and didn't know if it was in his body, and didn't know if he was out of his body the whole time he was there.*

-JOHN BEVERE

Everyday we believe and trust in things we can't see or prove. We live our lives without any guarantee of the future. We go to and fro unsure of what tomorrow will bring and not knowing what will come from all of our striving. God wants us to be successful, but it is important that we are not putting our hope and trust in things that will not last.

Scripture describes Heaven as a real place. Its existence is a reality that we can live by and focus on. It is a place of indescribable beauty and size. The Bible teaches this is the place that we, as believers, will live after death on this earth. As believers we do not just *believe* in Christ, we *know* Him by His Word and Spirit and by genuine experience.

God's promises are for us today, and His promise of having a heavenly dwelling place after death can be a source of great hope and joy throughout our time on earth. It is what being driven by eternity means for the believer, the over-comer. Give some serious thought to the promise of heaven and what you are living for. Let the Lord reveal what things you are putting your trust in that can be replaced by things of eternity.

Will you trust God, His Son, and Spirit when they speak to you of heaven and hell, the things that matter for all of eternity?

## Week 6 · Day 2

*"Most people that have experienced heaven, I have learned that they said they did not want to come back."*

-JOHN BEVERE

"I know a man in Christ who fourteen years ago was caught up to the third heaven. Whether it was in the body or out of the body I do not know – God knows. And I know that this man – whether in the body or apart from the body I do not know, but God knows – was caught up to paradise. He heard inexpressible things that man is not permitted to tell."

-Paul the Apostle, in 2 Corinthians 12:2-4

The apostle Paul was highly educated in the Scripture and in religious law. He was a devout leader and persecutor of those who chose to follow Jesus. He probably could recite the Law of Moses and portions of what is now the Old Testament before his conversion. But all of his knowledge couldn't have prepared him for a journey to Heaven.

When you catch sight of what God has promised us for all of eternity, your life will change. When this promise is buried deep in your heart and you know it to be true, you will begin to live for another reason. You will live to spend eternity in heaven, the place where you will be face to face with God. The things of this life will grow "strangely dim" in the light of the promise of heaven.

Paul's trip to heaven was still affecting his life fourteen years later, at the writing of 2 Corinthians, and beyond that. It was what he lived for, and he knew the promise would be fulfilled. Tirelessly preaching, teaching, working, praying, giving and caring, Paul knew what his life was for and where his priorities lay. We have the same promise today and it can have the same affect on our lives.

How we live our lives now, will affect how we live in eternity…Are you focused on receiving heavenly dwellings?

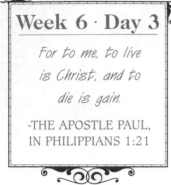

## Week 6 · Day 3

*For to me, to live is Christ, and to die is gain.*

-THE APOSTLE PAUL, IN PHILIPPIANS 1:21

Have you thought of the heavenly place where we will spend eternity? What about those we will be spending eternity with? The King of Kings, and all those who were created to worship Him! We will meet those from our family that have gone before us, not only grandparents and great-grandparents, but every individual that believed and followed the ways of Christ throughout our family history. We will stand among the thousands upon thousands of angels to worship for all of eternity.

But you have come to Mount Zion, to the heavenly Jerusalem, the city of the living God. You have come to the thousands upon thousands of angels in joyful assembly, to the church of the first born, whose names are written in heaven. You have come to God, the judge of all men, to the spirits of righteous men made perfect, to Jesus the mediator of a new covenant, and to the sprinkled blood that speaks a better word then the blood of Abel.

-Hebrews 12:22-26

Imagine before you the throne of God, the judge of all men. And at His right hand Jesus, who has been your mediator and has been 'ever living to make intercession' for you. You will then know that no other has saved you, no other focus has been worthwhile, except that which was of God.

Standing among the great men and women of faith, there will be no envy. You will not wish you had been like another, for you will know perfectly what God called you to. With all faces focused on the throne of God, you will be overcome with thankfulness and joy. The very things that you could not imagine here on earth, streets paved with pure gold, the size of the heavenly city, the very face of God, will be there before you for all of eternity.

Is it worth living a life that counts today? Is it worth the words of the Apostle Paul in Philippians 1:21, "For to me, to live is Christ, and to die is gain"?

We have an opportunity today to make decisions that will last forever and 'echo in eternity.' What decisions do you find it hard to make? Now is the time to pray and ask for the grace of God that will empower you to live as he has called you everyday, and in every decision.

## Week 6 · Day 4

*...there are two residences for believers who've died. The present home is referred to by most as **heaven**, but is scripturally referred to as **the heavenly** Jerusalem.*

-JOHN BEVERE

Heaven is the place at this time where believers go when they pass on. But who – if anyone else – dwells there, in this very real *heavenly Jerusalem*? We get a glimpse in Hebrews 12:22-24:

> But you have come to Mount Zion and to the city of the living God, the heavenly Jerusalem, to an innumerable company of angels, to the general assembly and church of the firstborn *who are* registered in heaven, to God the Judge of all, to the spirits of just men made perfect, to Jesus the Mediator of the new covenant, and to the blood of sprinkling that speaks better things than *that of* Abel.

Here we see that the Father and Son are there, as well as countless angels. The general assembly and the church of the firstborn reside there too, as are the Old Testament saints and those in Christ who have passed on. Jesus is called the firstborn of many brethren (Rom. 8:29).

And there is another group mentioned here as well. Notice "the *spirits* of just men made perfect" are found in this city. Who are these people, since the writer has already covered both the Old and New Testament saints who've gone on to their reward?

Remember that when we are born again by the Spirit of God, we become new creations; our spirits are made perfect in the likeness of Christ. In this verse the writer does not refer to their souls or bodies, but only their spirits. Could it be this speaks of the saints here on earth serving Jesus? Think of it: Hebrews says "Let us therefore come boldly to the throne of grace" (4:16). The throne of grace is located in the midst of the city of God, and this invitation is spoken to us who are on earth. Because our spirits have been created in the image of God and we have been born again, we now have the availability through the blood of Jesus and power of the Holy Spirit to go into the throne room of God anytime we have need or we desire to worship.

Could it be that many who yet live here on earth are well known in the throne room because they come often through prayer? How incredibly exciting that you may join them even now! What would the Lord have you bring to the throne room today?

## Week 6 · Day 5

*The final home of the righteous will also be called Jerusalem, but it will be located on earth. This is the city that will come down from heaven after the final judgment. It is called the New Jerusalem (Rev. 21:2).*

-JOHN BEVERE

Once the existing heavens and earth are purged by fire (2 Pet. 3:10-13), the New Heaven and New Earth will emerge. The Apostle John writes, "I saw a new heaven and a new earth for the first heaven and the first earth had passed away" (Rev. 21:1). This will be the final dwelling place of the believers who've passed on. It will be home to all the ransomed of the Lord from Adam to those received into glory at Christ's second coming.

These glorified saints will live in the city of God, the New Jerusalem. They'll receive their rewards and eternal positions of service to the Eternal King prior to the Millennium at the Judgment Seat of Christ.

John's description is that of a takes-your-breath-away wondrous place like no earthly city we have ever seen. Jasper, pearl and gold so pure it is transparent are just some of the amazing characteristics of this world. It will be filled with the glory of God and emanate opulence, radiance, and splendor. There will be no sickness, no death, no tears and no corruption whatsoever because it is utterly pure. Isaiah 65:25 says *the wolf and the lamb shall feed together, The lion shall eat straw like the ox.*

Besides the amazing things we've mentioned here, notice Scripture points out something else that is beyond even these. *We will see His face.* What Moses longed for and was denied we will behold. How awesome and exciting!

And there shall be no more curse, but the throne of God and of the Lamb shall be in it, and His servants shall serve Him. They shall see His face, and His name shall be on their foreheads.

-Revelation 22:3-4

When you think of the splendors of the new heaven and earth, and beholding the Lord's face, how does this inspire you?

_____

_____

_____

_____

_____

_____

_____

## Week 6 · Day 6

*Only the redeemed of Christ with glorified bodies will reside in the New Jerusalem; however, it appears from Scripture that those in natural bodies will be able to traffic through and partake of the fruit and worship the Lord. This is seen in John's writings. **The nations of the earth will walk in its [The New Jerusalem's] light, and the rulers of the world will come and bring their glory to it. Its gates never close at the end of day because there is no night. And all the nations will bring their glory and honor into the city.** (Revelation 21:24-26, NLT).*

-JOHN BEVERE

A nd he showed me a pure river of water of life, clear as crystal, proceeding from the throne of God and of the Lamb. In the middle of its street, and on either side of the river, was the tree of life, which bore twelve fruits, each tree yielding its fruit every month. The leaves of the tree were for the *healing of the nations*...There shall be no night there: They need no lamp nor light of the sun, for the Lord God gives them light. And *they shall reign forever and ever.*
-Revelation 22:1,2,5 (emphasis added)

Notice that the leaves of the tree of life bring healing to *the nations*. This begs interesting questions. *Who* will comprise these nations since the saints dwell in the city? Who will the saints reign over forever? Isaiah provides some insight. This is not a passage about the millennial reign of Christ for it is when the new heaven and earth are already in place.

Look! I am creating new heavens and a new earth – so wonderful that no one will even think about the old ones anymore. Be glad; rejoice forever in my creation! And look! I will create Jerusalem as a place of happiness. Her people [the redeemed saints] will be a source of joy. I will rejoice in Jerusalem and delight in my people. And the sound of weeping and crying will be heard no more. [Now Isaiah turns to people outside the New Jerusalem] No longer will babies die when only a few days old. No longer will adults die before they have lived a full life. No longer will people be considered old at one hundred! Only sinners will die that young! In those days, people will live in the houses they build and eat the fruit of their own vineyards. It will not be like the past, when invaders took the houses and confiscated the vineyards. For my people will live as long as trees and will have time to enjoy their hard-won gains. They will not work in vain, and their children will not be doomed to misfortune. For they are people blessed by the Lord, and their children, too, will be blessed.

-Isaiah 65:17-23 (NLT)

From the Apostle John and Isaiah, it appears that there will be people who live outside the city building their own homes in an everlasting time of peace and prosperity. This couldn't be the saints residing in the holy city, for they already have mansions prepared for them by Jesus (John 14:2-4). Also there will be children. This couldn't refer to the glorified saints because Jesus made it clear that they would not give birth to babies, for they'll not marry (Matt. 22:30). Perhaps these nations will inhabit the new earth, enriching it with planting, harvesting, and building. They multiply and replenish the Earth unhindered thus fulfilling God's original design; just as Adam and his seed would have if he had not fallen!

Have you ever thought of heaven like this before?

# Week 6 · Day 7

*When she [Mary] saw Jesus in His resurrected body He didn't look like a sci-fi alien. She mistook Him for the gardener. So, you know what that tells me? He looked just like a human being. He had a very similar body to ours and it wasn't until He said, "Mary," and she heard His voice that she recognized Him.*

-JOHN BEVERE

Revelation describes heaven as a place of indescribable majesty, perfection, fantastic glory, and beauty. It has waters of life, the throne of God, the Lamb of God, angels, and mansions prepared for us by Jesus Himself (John 14:2-4). With perfect peace, no sickness, no tears, and no death, it is a place so beyond what we could ask or think, unimaginable in its grandeur, and the fulfillment of our deepest desires and longings. We will have wondrous lives there and will worship God for eternity.

But what will *we* be like? What happens to the Christian who has died and gone to heaven? Let's look to the Scriptures for some insight.

After He was resurrected, the Lord appeared to Mary. She mistook Him for the gardener; He therefore had a body that is very similar to what we possess. She didn't recognize Him for she couldn't dare believe He was alive. She saw Him brutally slain, carried away, and buried. It wasn't until He spoke to her personally that she could believe it was really Him. Later Jesus appeared to His disciples. He said, "Why are you troubled? And why do doubts arise in your hearts? Behold My hands and My feet, that it is I Myself. Handle Me and see, for a spirit does not have flesh and bones as you see I have" (Luke 24:38-39).

Jesus in His resurrection body had flesh and bones, and He ate food (Luke 24:41-43), walked, talked, floated through the air (when He ascended to heaven), walked through walls with locked doors (John 20:19), could vanish from sight, and travel instantaneously wherever He chose (Luke 24:31).

Believers too will be given new bodies and will be able to do some amazing things just like Jesus. He was the firstborn among many brethren, and we shall be in the likeness of His resurrection:

For if we have been united together in the likeness of His death, certainly we also shall be in the likeness of His resurrection.

-ROMANS 6:5

Beloved, now are we the sons of God, and it doth not yet appear what we shall be: but we know that, when he shall appear, we shall be like him; for we shall see him as he is.

-1 JOHN 3:2, KJV

...and from Jesus Christ, the faithful witness, the firstborn from the dead, and the ruler over the kings of the earth. To Him who loved us and washed us from our sins in His own blood...

-REVELATION 1:5

For whom He foreknew, He also predestined to be conformed to the image of His Son, that He might be the firstborn among many brethren.

-ROMANS 8:29

Certainly heaven is a place beyond our wildest hopes and dreams!

### *Driven by Eternity:*
## YOUR WEEK IN REVIEW

- Heaven is a very real place.

- Paul the Apostle himself testified about it.

- To live is Christ and to die is gain.

- When believer's die they go to the heavenly Jerusalem.

- When you pray, you can boldly by grace go to the very throne room of God in heaven!

- The believer's final dwelling place is the New Jerusalem on the New Earth where we will reign over nations.

- The New Heaven and New Earth will be glorious beyond our best imaginations!

God wants us to have a blessed life on earth, serving Him and serving others in the power of His Spirit. When we do this, we get a foretaste of heaven, which naturally gives us a longing for it. Torn between heaven and Earth, we are to give our lives completely to Jesus. We can be content in the knowledge that He will not fail to love us, bless us, and keep us when we do this!

- What are *you* thinking and feeling right now about all this?

- Are there other Scriptures about these amazing truths that are coming to your mind?

- How do previous teachings from your past fit in with it all?

- What is God saying about how He can help you now in your life as you seek to live driven by eternity?

Pray and journal in your own words, letting the Lord minister to you. He desires you to experience great strength, freedom, and joy in His Spirit and Word!

# The Breathtaking Glories and Wonders of Heaven

*But as it is written: "Eye has not seen, nor ear heard, nor have entered into the heart of man the things which God has prepared for those who love Him."*
*-1 CORINTHIANS 2:9*

1. As you think on 1 Corinthians 2:9, how does that Scripture fit with the many amazing truths John Bevere brings forth in this hour?

2. In heaven we receive glorified bodies and can do many amazing things. What are some examples? Can you think of the Scriptures that go along with them?

3. Besides believers, who dwells there right now?

4. In what truly wondrous ways may believers be spiritually present in heaven while still alive and well on earth?

**hot TOPIC** John Bevere gives the account of his friend's son, the boy who was electrocuted and went to heaven, only to be called back by his father through intense prayer. Yet when he able to go back to his family he was disappointed. How do you feel about some of the amazing things he experienced in heaven? Are they scriptural?

**The Saints rule and reign in an all new heaven and earth.**

*God reversed man's defeat into a blessing by gathering out of fallen mankind a glorified heavenly people — that would be saints, you and I — through Christ's redemption who would eventually reign over humanity in the new earth. This helps understand Jesus' words, to the faithful steward,* "Well done good and faithful servants. Because you were faithful in very little have authority over 10 cities." *Luke 19:17.*

-JOHN BEVERE

5.  What is Revelations 21:10,11 describing:

    So he took me in spirit to a great, high mountain, and he showed me the holy city, Jerusalem, descending out of heaven from God. It was filled with the glory of God and sparkled like a precious gem, crystal clear like jasper.

    _____

Once the existing heavens and earth are purged by fire (2 Pet. 3:10-13), the new heaven and new earth will emerge. The apostle John writes, "I saw a new heaven and a new earth, for the first heaven and the first earth had passed away" (Rev. 21:1). No longer will anything be cursed.

Only the redeemed of Christ with glorified bodies will reside in the New Jerusalem; however, it appears from Scripture that there will also be a people who have natural bodies who will be able to traffic through and partake of the fruit and worship the Lord:

The nations of the earth will walk in its [The New Jerusalem's] light, and the rulers of the world will come and bring their glory to it. Its gates never close at the end of day because there is no night. And all the nations will bring their glory and honor into the city.

-Revelation 21:24-26, NLT.

And he showed me a pure river of water of life, clear as crystal, proceeding from the throne of God and of the Lamb. In the middle of its street, and on either side of the river, was the tree of life, which bore twelve fruits, each tree yielding its fruit every month. The leaves of the tree were for the *healing of the nations…* There shall be no night there: They need no lamp nor light of the sun, for the Lord God gives them light. And *they shall reign forever and ever.*

-Revelation 22:1,2,5 (emphasis added)

6.  What important questions do the words *"the nations"* and *"they shall reign forever and ever"* pose?

    _____

Look! I am creating new heavens and a new earth – so wonderful that no one will even think about the old ones anymore. Be glad; rejoice forever in my creation! And look! I will create Jerusalem as a place of happiness. Her people [the redeemed saints] will be a source of joy. I will rejoice in Jerusalem and delight in my people. And the sound of weeping and crying will be heard no more. [Now Isaiah turns to people outside the New Jerusalem] No longer will babies die when only a few days old. No longer will adults die before they have lived a full life. No longer will people be considered old at one hundred! Only sinners will die that young! In those days, people will live in the houses they build and eat the fruit of their own vineyards. It will not be like the past, when invaders took the houses and confiscated the vineyards. For my people will live as long as trees and will have time to enjoy their hard-won gains. They will not work in vain, and their children will not be doomed to misfortune. For they are people blessed by the Lord, and their children, too, will be blessed.

-Isaiah 65:17-23 (NLT)

To learn some of what life will be like in the New Heaven and Earth, read the passages from the Apostle John (Revelation 22:1,2,5 and 21:24-26, NLT) and Isaiah 65:17-23 above.

7.  It seems that there will be people who live outside the city of New Jerusalem, building their own homes in an everlasting time of peace and prosperity. Who will this be?

8.  Also there will be children. Whose children are they?

9.  Perhaps these nations will inhabit the new earth unhindered, enriching it with planting, harvesting, and building. Why would God have them multiply and replenish the Earth?

10. How could it be that these were people from the millennium, who then live blessed eternal lives in un-glorified bodies, and whom the glorified saints will reign over forever and ever?

## Hell's lesson?

There is a place in the New Heaven and Earth that people are going to be able to look down and see the tormented souls that are being burned in hell forever and ever in the lake of fire (Isa. 66:22-24). Could God, in His wisdom, have said, "I'm going to do this to be a strong deterrent from people rebelling against Me?"

11. What do these astounding truths mean to you in your heart and mind right now?

12. What do these truths mean to you in your daily walk with God? Are there things you need to "clean up" or do by His grace and power? Does it motivate you? Bring godly fear?

13. What do they mean to you in your desire and ability to be His witness?

## Heaven's worth!

There is a riveting account in the New Testament of a man of faith who was martyred. He worked great miracles, and as he preached just before his death, his face shone as an angel.

> But he, being full of the Holy Spirit, gazed into heaven and saw the glory of God, and Jesus standing at the right hand of God, and said, "Look! I see the heavens opened and the Son of Man standing at the right hand of God!"
>
> -ACTS 7:55-56

14. Who was this, right before he was about to be stoned to death by an angry mob?

15. What very important person was in the crowd observing this and consenting to the death of this martyr?

16. Do you think heaven is worth enduring such a terrible death?

God works all things together for good in amazing ways! Remember that later in his life Paul was taken by God on a visit to Heavenly Jerusalem (heaven).

17. Do you think perhaps Paul recalled the stoning of Stephen, and how do you think Paul was impacted by this event? Would it have helped cause him to live a life driven by eternity? Why?

**ZENITH**
the time when
something is
most powerful
or successful.

This has been a truly breathtaking tour of heaven! What is the overwhelming "big idea" in this session that you can take away from this forever?

How can you take it and use it to influence others for Jesus?

# The Judgment Seat of Christ

## HOUR 7

Please refer to Chapter 10,

The Judgment Seat of Christ,

in the *Driven by Eternity* book

and video session 7.

## Week 7 · Day 1

*For we shall all stand before the judgment seat of Christ. For it is written: "As I live, says the LORD, every knee shall bow to Me, and every tongue shall confess to God."*

-THE APOSTLE PAUL,
IN ROMANS 14:10-11

The Book of Romans is the most complete and systematic of Paul's teachings; it also reveals much about him as a man of God. It was written to give some important teaching that the church at Rome very much needed. Comprised of both Jews and Gentiles, the mix of people in the church made for varying lifestyles, beliefs, values, and doctrines. Paul wrote to correct errors and reconcile differences…to bring understanding and harmony.

The Scriptures are the Word of God. Given by inspiration of the Holy Spirit, they are God talking to us. Paul may have been the messenger, but the message was signed by God Himself.

Paul was letting the believers at Rome know for certain that all would face God in judgment. He would say the same to you in your church today.

The apostle includes himself in his declaration. "We all" means **everybody** will stand before the King of all kings, the righteous and all-powerful Judge.

Appearing before a judge is something most people who are going about their daily lives don't think too much about. But most get pretty nervous when they see red flashing lights behind them while they are driving along in their cars. Even something as minor as a parking violation can bring you before a judge and cause you to be anxious for weeks preceding your appearance.

Now think for a moment about appearing before God Almighty, with your whole life at stake, for all of eternity without end. Nervous? **You are already scheduled to appear before God, in His court!** No exceptions, no plea bargains, no appeals. The decision of the Judge will be final and set in stone for eternity.

Are you ready to stand before God as judge? If not, what can you do now to prepare for that day?

_____

_____

_____

_____

_____

_____

_____

_____

_____

## Week 7 · Day 2

*It is safe to say that there has never been a more unfair, illegal, or shameful set of trials conducted in the history of jurisprudence than the six trials that led to the crucifixion and death of the Lord Jesus Christ. In this, however, there is a paradox: From those acts of injustice, the justice of God was satisfied!*

-CHARLES SWINDOLL

Jesus lived a life immersed in people's lives. It is why He came. He came for you...He came for all people. The object of ridicule and contempt, He was scorned because He spent quality time with sinners of all kinds. He also spent time with powerful religious people, with soldiers and business people. Children laughed and played on His knee, and He went to a wedding celebration. He was a carpenter, a man with tough hands and an eye for a straight edge. He wasn't afraid to get His hands dirty or His brow wet with sweat. Jesus wasn't necessarily concerned about what folks thought or what was considered status quo.

What *was* Jesus concerned about? Love, truth, righteousness, salvation, heaven, and judgment. He came willingly to do His Father's bidding and to glorify God, all the while walking perfectly in the Holy Spirit.

Jesus may have gotten His hands soiled, His feet worn and dusty, His heart wrenched and body broken as He toiled among sinners, the poor and diseased, thieves, religious hypocrites, evil politicians and ruthless soldiers – but never was His heart polluted. Tempted in all points just as we are, as Hebrews 4:15 says, never did He yield to sin. Never did He give in to the pressures of the lusts of the flesh, of the world system, or the temptations of Satan.

The only person who ever lived among us without any sin at all, much less any illegal deed, was unfairly tried (several times in different ways), falsely judged, brutally tortured, and finally executed with no just cause at all.

On the other hand, there is plenty of cause to condemn any of us. We who are born into sin, who live lives with countless infractions, should be condemned to hell. But He forgives and saves us, Himself having borne the penalty of our sin.

And then in His rich mercy He has scheduled us to go before the one Judge we can trust, who is truly just, fair, and perfect in His judgments – Himself. At the Judgment Seat of Christ we will be rewarded according to how our lives endure the fire of God's standard. That which was equivalent to wood, hay, and stubble will be burned. Silver, gold and precious stones will remain.

**It is indeed amazing grace when the sinless and perfect Lord rewards us who were sinful and imperfect! How does this make you feel? Grateful? Wanting to serve the One who bore your judgment?**

_____

_____

_____

_____

_____

_____

1. Charles R. Swindoll, *The Darkness and the Dawn* (Nashville: W Publishing Group, 2001), 66.

## Week 7 · Day 3

*We read, "For to this end Christ died and rose and lived again, that He might be Lord of both the dead and the living. But why do you judge your brother?"*

*We're talking about believers here, not unbelievers. "Or why do you show contempt for your brother? For we shall all stand before the judgment seat of Christ."*

*(Rom. 14:9-10).*

-JOHN BEVERE

Christians need not fear death or eternity because they know where they are going. The question of entrance to heaven has been settled by their genuine relationship with the Lord. We who were once dead in sin but are now saved by grace live a life following Him in His footsteps. The degree to which we are or are not faithful will determine our level of reward at the Judgment Seat of Christ.

> For we must all appear before the judgment seat of Christ; that every one may receive the things done in his body, according to that he hath done, whether it be good or bad.
>
> -2 CORINTHIANS 5:10, KJV

**The Great Exchange.** Jesus did not deserve the trials, tortures, and gruesome crucifixion He endured. We too will get what we don't deserve – but in the complete opposite sense. We deserve to be convicted, but we get off. We should be condemned and receive the horrible penalty of hell. But instead, because of Jesus' unfair treatment and His sacrifice on our behalf, we get into heaven and receive eternal life with God. And then on top of that we get to be blessed with rewards!

You get into heaven strictly on Jesus' merit, not your own. But at the Judgment Seat you are judged for your God-given responsibilities as a believer, and everything you did is going to come to light. Were you obedient to the Word? Did you share your faith? Did you reach out to the poor, the widow, and the imprisoned? How did you steward the gifts and talents God gave you?

Only believers will stand here. Your life has been under God's microscope. No word or deed has gone unnoticed. All will be carefully examined on that day. And you who deserved to be condemned to eternal torment will instead receive eternal blessings in accordance with how your life held up to God's measure.

Take a moment to thank God for His great mercy and love for you in this great exchange! Are you just living, or are you living in your calling, according to God's measure for your life each day?

**Week 7 · Day 4**

*"None of these things move me; nor do I count my life dear to myself..."*

-ACTS 20:24

I t is easier to serve or work for God without a vision and without a call, because then you are not bothered by what He requires. Common sense, covered with a layer of Christian emotion, becomes your guide. You may be more prosperous and successful from the world's perspective, and will have more leisure time, if you never acknowledge the call of God. But once you receive a commission from Jesus Christ, the memory of what God asks of you will always be there to prod you on to do His will. You will no longer be able to work for Him on the basis of common sense. Never consider whether or not you are of use – but always consider that "you are not your own." (1 Corinthians 6:19)

You are His.[1]

-OSWALD CHAMBERS

"You are not your own." That is surely a countercultural statement. If there is a priority message in today's society, it is that you *are* your own. From cola commercials to the Supreme Court, Western civilization is built on that premise in many ways. But not the eternal kingdom of God. You've been bought with a price. And you will find the more you hold your life dear to yourself, the more things slip away. But as you give your life to Him, His call will grow daily in you, and so will His equipping power. You will find He meets you in faith and is with you as you go about His business.

Many find this difficult to believe. But He does it all because we are His. To accept that Jesus is truly the lover of our souls is almost more than we can take in.

The sound of those words brings hope. We are taken aback by them, startled by them, but deep down inside, way within us, we hope. Could it be true? "*He* could really love *me* and call me His own? I am *His*?" YES. You are. It's that simple.

But it wasn't simple to get you there. You are purchased with His very life, suffering, and blood sacrifice. That is the very reason you can most assuredly believe you are His beloved. You can settle that in your spirit and sigh in blessed relief and rejoice in it. And then make Him yours. The Song of Solomon puts it like this: "I am my beloved's, and my beloved is mine" (Song of Sol. 6:3).

From the heavenly mountains, from God's gates and hills He calls to you. "Come, be with Me. Love Me and follow Me. There is more to your life than you ever imagined!" You are not your own. You are His. Will you make Him yours? Will you say yes to the One who gave Himself for you? It's a call to higher things, to follow His ways, catch His vision, capture His heart. These are what bring you to fulfill His desire for you. These are what prepare you for the Judgment Seat of Christ. But here is a "secret" to it all:

**It's easy to have confidence at the Judgment Seat when you are going to meet with the love of your life.** Are you His, living in that secret place? What is the Holy Spirit is saying to you?

1. Oswald Chambers, *My Utmost for His Highest Devotional* (Oswald Chambers Publications Association, LTD, 1992), s.v. "March 4."

# Week 7 · Day 5

*If you take a million, you divide it by infinity, it's zero. If you take eighty years, let's say you live to be eighty years old and you divide it by infinity, it's zero. This life is zero. Whatever we do in this zero time determines how we're going to spend eternity. Not where. As a believer where is settled by our receiving Jesus Christ as our Lord and Master and Savior. That's settled. But how we spend "infinity" is determined by this zero time.*

-JOHN BEVERE

I f our faith is about anything, it is about how we live in the empowerment of God's grace. The place where the rubber meets the road – the daily practical application – is the very place we should shine. The apostle John said we are overcomers in life because of Christ in us. "You are of God, little children, and have overcome them, because He who is in you is greater than he who is in the world" (1 John 4:4). And look at what James says:

> Come now, you who say, "Today or tomorrow we will go to such and such a city, spend a year there, buy and sell, and make a profit"; whereas you do not know what will happen tomorrow. For what is your life? It is even a vapor that appears for a little time and then vanishes away.
>
> -JAMES 4:13-14

The Book of James shows the necessity of having a living, vital faith. Faith that is not lived out in our lives is worthless.

John and James are trying to tell us something radical, something revolutionary to our existence. We can thrive, not just survive, in our time on earth if we'll have ears to hear. What are these bold preachers trying to communicate?

Life is short, so make the most of it. Do this by radical faith in following Jesus. Radical faith says, "Life is short, so spend it on Jesus." This is opposed to today's prevailing philosophy that says, "Life is short, so spend it on yourself."

James has news for us all. Spending your life on yourself is mostly a sad waste! You don't know what will happen minutes from now, let alone what is going to take place tomorrow. But there is one who does know, and furthermore He holds it all in the palm of His hand. Live His way, His plan, His vision, and His heart, and you end up at the end of the day – and at the end of your life – having made a difference.

**Life is short. Make yours count today and forever. How is God showing you to do this?**

_____

_____

_____

_____

*Scientists prove time flies when you're busy!*

-PRESS RELEASE,
UNIVERSITY OF
ALBERTA, CANADA,
AUGUST 6, 2004

It appears the more attention a task requires the faster time flies. Most today would agree that the basics of daily life – work and family – take the bulk of our concentration. Life's details can rapidly consume your time, and before you know it, life goes faster than we can keep up with. Then suddenly...time's up.

Ask any husband or wife. Just finding the time to balance the checkbook properly is a real challenge. Ask a serious college student if he has enough time to balance the rigors of campus life. Ask children if they have enough time to play...grandpas and grandmas if they have enough time left to live out their dreams...lovers if they have enough time to love. Life moves pretty fast.

The other side of the coin is worth a look too. Ask a prisoner if time seems to be flying by...or the person who is hospitalized in pain...or the spouse of a soldier anxiously waiting for a return from war.

How about when you lose a loved one? Doesn't time seem to crawl as you plunge the depths of grief and sorrow? Relief cannot come fast enough when times are bad.

If you think about that, you realize how important eternity is. No one wants awful times to last a split second more than necessary. That's a pretty good reason to make sure you are not in danger of a torturous eternity!

For the faithful believer, heaven is home, so the "where" of eternity is not really the issue. It's the "way" you are going to spend that eternity that is now paramount. Life speeds by. Here today, gone tomorrow, you wake up at thirty...forty...sixty...eighty years of age and think, *Where did it all go? What did I do with the time?*

Do you think of eternity throughout your busy day? Usually, most do not; however, what you do today will have an eternal impact in heaven and in someone's life. The way you're going to spend eternity – infinity – is determined by how you live.

**Will you spend your time differently?**

1. "Scientists Prove Time Flies When You're Busy," University of Alberta (Canada) press release, http://www.eurekalert.org/pub_releases/2004-08/uoa-spt080604.php (accessed February 6, 2006).

## Week 7 · Day 7

*This is where it really gets to people. Not only are you going to be judged by your words and your works, but your thoughts and your motives are going to be examined as well.*

-JOHN BEVERE

This is a startling concept that really raises people's attention levels. "You mean everything?" they ask. Yes, everything we say and do, along with the motives behind them, will be judged. Having been under God's careful scrutiny, nothing will be overlooked or "winked at." So we better not deceive others or ourselves.

The truth, of course, is that the life we live before others, and even how we perceive ourselves, may be vastly different than the realities that lie within our hearts.

We may fool people some of the time, ourselves included for sure, but never God. Believers who stay in God's Word and involved in a good local fellowship build a reliable conscience. When their heart or actions are not in line with God's Word, they see their own sin and repent. Obedience at all costs, no matter the circumstance, is the rule of their heart.

On the other hand, many people live in a downward spiral – some fast and obvious, others slowly and barely noticed – slipping further into the dull blur between fantasy and reality, truth and lies. They eventually end up with a heart full of wrong motives and often essentially evil intentions. "Large" or "small" evils are not the point. Though too many of these people may appear "just fine," God knows differently.

What can we do? How do we know we are not deceiving our own hearts and minds? How do we know our motives, intentions, words, and deeds are pure? It seems like a pretty tall order. Can a person even attain to such lofty ideals?

Yes. Never fear, God has supplied our needs in all things of life and godliness. Hebrews 4:12 (NLT) gives us the answer:

> For the word of God is full of living power. It is sharper than the sharpest knife, cutting deep into our innermost thoughts and desires. It exposes us for what we really are.

The believer who is following God's Word and obeying His commands can know the truth, because the Word is the just and impartial judge of our hearts and actions. We may judge falsely, but when we compare our hearts and minds, words and deeds to the plumb line of God's statutes, the guesswork is removed. The building we're erecting on the Word of truth will be straight and strong if we follow the Architect's design.

Every moment of every day we have two simple but major choices. We will either gravitate to the flesh, or we will gravitate toward the Spirit. The flesh is likened to wood, hay, and stubble that will be burned up in judgment. The Spirit is eternal, which is like gold, silver, and precious stones, and for these you are rewarded. For each situation we face, God supplies an answer if we will choose Him.

Is this legalism or paranoia? No, it is about *relationship*. It is about trust, love, and desiring to please the One who loves you and gave Himself for you. And it goes much deeper than the examples given above. Life is complex, and we are inventive and creative when it comes to excusing our thought-life and our actions. But this is as plain and straightforward as it gets. You are saved, and God says a lot of things about how you are to live your life as His child.

When you stack your conduct up against your profession of faith, what is the Holy Spirit saying to you about it? Again, this is not legalism, but about loving the One you say you love.

_____

_____

_____

_____

*Driven by Eternity:*
## YOUR WEEK IN REVIEW

- All believers will stand before the Judgment Seat of Christ.

- You are already scheduled to meet Him there! Only He knows when.

- Truly God has given us amazing grace. Jesus was sinless but received our penalty; we were guilty and get heaven's rewards!

- Time flies! Our life is but a vapor; it is zero compared to eternity.

- The way we live now, in this life, determines how we will spend eternity.

The way to remove fear of the judgment is to have an intimate relationship with the judge! God has given us the right and ability to know our just Judge and prepare for that day! Read again this sentence from day 4: **It's easy to have confidence at the Judgment Seat when you are going to meet with the love of your life.**

Imagine meeting Christ at the Judgment Seat in two scenarios.

1.) You know Him as Savior, but you are fearful to actually meet Him because you have no idea what He is really like.

2.) You have walked intimately with Him, followed His ways, and been immersed in His Word and Spirit, living life by His leading and His power.

Describe the feelings you get in each of these scenarios, and then write what the Lord is saying to you about your meeting Him on that great day.

_____

_____

_____

# LIFE IS SHORT

*For your life is like the morning fog – it's here a little while, then it's gone.*
*-JAMES 4:14, NLT*

---

1. It's not just anybody saying this. When God Himself tells you that life is short, here and then gone, what does that mean to you?

   _____

   _____

   _____

2. How does James 4:14 affect your feelings toward others – family, friends, co-workers, both saved and unsaved?

   _____

   _____

   _____

An epitaph is a short literary piece written about the life of a deceased person. It is what would be engraved on a tombstone. Here are examples of what could be two very different "epitaphs" from the Bible:

- **King Saul:** "And Samuel said unto Saul, I will not return with thee: for thou hast rejected the word of the LORD, and the LORD hath rejected thee from being king over Israel" (1 Sam. 15:26, KJV).

- **King David:** "And when he had removed him (Saul), he raised up unto them David to be their king; to whom also he gave testimony, and said, I have found David the son of Jesse, a man after mine own heart, which shall fulfill all my will" (Acts 13:22, KJV).

3. If your life were over today, how would your epitaph read?

   _____

   _____

   _____

4. How would you like it to read?

   _____

   _____

   _____

5.  When you think of this, are there things you want to change or do in your life before your life is finished?

_____

_____

_____

The purpose of the Book of James is not to lament that life is short, but to encourage us to live a life of *faith in action*. It is about putting feet to your faith and living dynamically in intimate relationship with the Lord Jesus.

6.  Think practically. *How can you incorporate the lessons you learn from the questions above into real daily living?* (Don't underestimate God's grace or the Holy Spirit when considering this.)

_____

_____

_____

## God cares greatly for you and your work

First Corinthians has a lot to say about how you can live a great and blessed life in the Lord. One of the best ways to seek and find the Lord is to look at His Word sentence by sentence and glean as much as possible, letting Him speak to you as you do so.

Read 1 Corinthians 9:24-27 sentence by sentence, and then write the things God shows you about what each powerful sentence is saying to you about how to "run the race" and win!:

*Do you not know that those who run in a race all run, but one receives the prize?*

_____

*Run in such a way that you may obtain it.*

_____

*And everyone who competes for the prize is temperate in all things.*

_____

*Now they do it to obtain a perishable crown, but we for an imperishable crown.*

_____

*Therefore I run thus: not with uncertainty.*

_____

*Thus I fight: not as one who beats the air.*

_____

*But I discipline my body and bring it into subjection, lest, when I have preached to others, I myself should become disqualified.*

_____

> For we are God's fellow workers; you are God's field, you are God's building. According to the grace of God which was given to me, as a wise master builder I have laid the foundation, and another builds on it. But let each one take heed how he builds on it. For no other foundation can anyone lay than that which is laid, which is Jesus Christ. Now if anyone builds on this foundation with gold, silver, precious stones, wood, hay, straw, each one's work will become clear; for the Day will declare it, because it will be revealed by fire; and the fire will test each one's work, of what sort it is. If anyone's work which he has built on it endures, he will receive a reward. If anyone's work is burned, he will suffer loss; but he himself will be saved, yet so as through fire.
>
> -1 CORINTHIANS 3:9-15

7.  How is our life compared to a building? How should we build, and what does it mean for your eternity?

_____

_____

> For the word of God is full of living power. It is sharper than the sharpest knife, cutting deep into our innermost thoughts and desires. It exposes us for what we really are.
>
> -HEBREWS 4:12, NLT

 Read each statement below.

> For we must all appear before the judgment seat of Christ; that every one may receive the things done in his body, according to that he hath done, whether it be good or bad.
>
> -2 CORINTHIANS 5:10, KJV

There are numerous individuals in the church unaware that they will give an account of what they've done in their short stay on the earth. Many have the erroneous idea that all future judgment is eradicated by their salvation. Indeed the blood of Jesus cleanses us from sins that would have kept us from the kingdom. However, it does not exempt us from the judgment of how we conduct ourselves as believers, whether good or bad. Now, listen to me carefully, the decisions that are made at the Judgment Seat will be eternal. That means they will last forever and ever and ever.

-John Bevere

8.  God judges our idle words and actions, as well as penetrates deeper to our very motives and intentions. How does this make you feel?

_____

_____

9.  Explain what that verse means to you in light of how you live today and when you will stand before Jesus at the Judgment Seat.

_____

_____

_____

## The Best Invitation You Ever Received!

To end this session, read the phenomenal words below. Praise God for such a promise and wonderful invitation!

Everything that goes into a life of pleasing God has been miraculously given to us by getting to know, personally and intimately, the One who invited us to God. The best invitation we ever received! We were also given absolutely terrific promises to pass on to you – your tickets to participation in the life of God after you turned your back on a world corrupted by lust. So don't lose a minute in building on what you've been given, complementing your basic faith with good character, spiritual understanding, alert discipline, passionate patience, reverent wonder, warm friendliness, and generous love, each dimension fitting into and developing the others. With these qualities active and growing in your lives, no grass will grow under your feet, no day will pass without its reward as you mature in your experience of our Master Jesus.

-2 PETER 1:3-8, THE MESSAGE

10. Have you accepted this invitation to know God intimately and follow Him in all His ways for the adventure of a blessed life? What amazing things does this passage say have been given to you?

_____

_____

11. How excited does this passage make you, and how can you influence others with what you've experienced?

_____

_____

**ZENITH**
the time when something is most powerful or successful.

What was the one thing that really stood out to you in this session? What are you going to do about it in your own life?

_____

_____

_____

_____

HOUR

Please refer to Chapter 11,

God's Custom House,

in the *Driven by Eternity* book

and video session 8.

## Week 8 · Day 1

*The rewards that are given at the Judgment Seat will span a wide range. They will go anywhere from having everything you did burned up, all the way to reigning beside Christ for eternity.*

-JOHN BEVERE

Think of this. In the court of heaven you are standing before Jesus, your King and Savior. It's time for you to be judged for how you lived your life as a believer. Your life is shown at work, with your family and friends, at your church, and at recreation, too. What you did with your finances, how you felt and acted toward others, why you made the decisions you made, everything you said and did…and what you *didn't* do but were *supposed* to do according to God's plan for your life is shown as well!

Day after day is consumed like straw in fire, leaving little or nothing that had eternal value! And your rewards – for all of eternity – are small indeed.

What a sorrowful picture. And perhaps the most terrible thing about it is that it was a needless waste. It doesn't have to be that way, of course. It could have been a completely different experience. Rewards could have been plentiful. There could have been the fruit of a life lived in God's calling at work and play, at home and church. There could have been long lines of people who were touched by all you did – up front and behind the scenes – as you quietly went about your calling from God.

What is more chilling yet is that on top of the eternal rewards, *all along* you could have been living a better, more fulfilling life on earth, too, with more peace and godly contentment! So how can you make sure that this doesn't happen to you, with your life's work counting for nothing at the judgment?

But lay up for yourselves treasures in heaven, where neither moth nor rust destroys and where thieves do not break in and steal. For where your treasure is, there your heart will be also….But seek first the kingdom of God and His righteousness, and all these things shall be added to you.

-MATTHEW 6:20-21, 33

God must come first in your life. It's that simple. Ask yourself: "What is the driving force of my life? Would my family, friends, and co-workers say I lived like a person driven by eternity?"

_____

_____

_____

_____

_____

_____

## Week 8 · Day 2

*In regard to your calling, you will not be judged according to what you did, but rather what you were called to do.*

-JOHN BEVERE

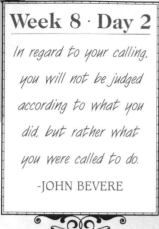

oday's opening statement definitely comes as a shock to most people. **God will judge believers according to what *He* calls you to do, not what you have done.** Many wrongly believe that God is going to judge whatever it is they are doing with their life. So they just live life that way, getting up in the morning, going through life's motions, and then doing it again, hoping it will all work out in the end. But that misses the whole point. God requires you to be doing what *He* has for you, and it is by *that* standard you will be judged.

What believers do here in their short time on earth determines how they will spend eternity. Just living is not the same as living in God's will. *The things you will do in heaven, the mansion you live in, the eternal rewards you receive will be according to whether or not you fulfilled what God called you to do.*

Your calling is everything, and when you find it and are living in it, it's easier to get up in the morning. There's a spring in your step and purpose in your days. The very life of God can flow through you in ways you may never have dreamed of. Sparks of creativity, insight, wisdom, and more will fly when you are fulfilling God's assignment for your life.

Are you living in your calling? Are you doing the things God has for you to do? Have you thought about your destiny or being rewarded in heaven for what you have done on earth? God calls us to be successful, but does God define success by the world's standards?

God had a perfect plan for you before you were born.

You saw me before I was born. Every day of my life was recorded in your book. Every moment was laid out before a single day had passed.

-PSALM 139:16, NLT

If you feel you have not been living in your calling, or perhaps you have never sought God for direction, it is never too late. Ask for forgiveness and earnestly seek Him now for what He has for you.

What is God speaking to you about His calling for your life at home? At work? In your local church?

## Week 8 · Day 3

*Our ability to build the kingdom of God is entirely based upon our cooperation with the Holy Spirit.*

-JOHN BEVERE

Cooperation means "working together with." We learn it at home, in kindergarten, and on through high school and college. Then we can carry the value of this into our own homes, the corporate world, and church.

Some learn the value of cooperation better than others. For those who want to achieve things in life, the absolute necessity of team, interpersonal, and cooperative skills becomes quickly apparent.

With the Lord, it is such an incredible privilege that we can even use the word. Who are we to be invited to cooperate with *God*?

But this is what He has planned from eternity past, now and forever. We get to be in a partnership with Him! He is Creator, God Almighty, and we are His creation. He has loved us and exalted us as His children. **He didn't have to, but God chose us and calls us to cooperate with the Holy Spirit.**

We are the ones who often tend to put more limits on our relationship than the Lord really has! He has given us His Word, and we are to join with Him and obey His calling for our life. He desires us to come into agreement with His will, to be filled with His Spirit, and to bear much fruit. As we do this, He gives us strength to meet difficulties, wisdom to handle life's situations, power to face challenges, and influence with others who need Him.

All the while He keeps a steady stream of His love, peace, contentment, and joy flowing into our spiritual veins as we seek Him and obey Him in all things of life. He has called us to partake of His divine nature, and His promises are multiplied to us!

Grace and peace be multiplied to you in the knowledge of God and of Jesus our Lord, as His divine power has given to us all things that pertain to life and godliness, through the knowledge of Him who called us by glory and virtue, by which have been given to us exceedingly great and precious promises, that through these you may be partakers of the divine nature.

-2 PETER 1:2-5

Glory, virtue, exceedingly great and precious promises! Pray this verse for yourself, letting God multiply His grace and peace to you. What are the areas you need more of God's grace in?

_____

_____

_____

_____

_____

## Week 8 · Day 4

*Christians increasingly live on a spiritual island; new and rival ways of life surround it in all directions and their tides come further up the beach every time.*[1]

-C. S. LEWIS

Those in the early church lived in a world full of persecution and suffering – no modern comforts or conveniences, no fast luxurious travel, no instant communication. But they had each other and the Holy Spirit, and they were about God's plans and purposes. Laboring amidst many difficulties, but with great power and a sense of destiny, people from all walks of life were called by God and fulfilled His will on earth.

*Therefore, my beloved brethren, be steadfast, immovable, always abounding in the work of the Lord, knowing that your labor is not in vain in the Lord.*

-1 Corinthians 15:58

In many ways we today have it better than our ancestors. But we still have plenty of challenges to our faith. The tides C. S. Lewis spoke of in 1958 continue to encroach on the church. There are new rivals, dangers, more voices, ideas, and choices than ever before. We need encouragement to hold fast to God's call on our lives and to the things that have eternal value.

We are to be in the world, though not of it. The island God provides is His kingdom, apart from the kingdom of this world. Delivered from the powers of darkness, we now live in the Kingdom of Jesus. The Holy Spirit is our oasis. Endless in resources, matchless in peace and tranquility, this is an island of beauty and power, from which we go out into the world and do God's work. Its beaches, though ever under siege from the world, will never be eroded away.

We need not tremble from the storms that rage. No, we tremble at His Word, and we follow the winds of His Spirit. We remain steadfast, immovable, empowered by His grace, continually abounding in the work of the Lord. We are influencers for Christ, and knowing the will of the Lord, we ever increase His kingdom as we live and preach the Word in our homes, at work, and at play.

Whether we live in a free and prosperous country, or in other much more difficult places on the earth, when things get tough, we remember God's Word and our brothers and sisters and those who went before us. Our "labor is not in vain in the Lord," and it will have eternal rewards.

**Wherever you are, whatever you do, be bold and strong, for your work matters to eternity!** In all you do, be encouraged today by the Holy Spirit, according to 1 Corinthians 15:58.

1. C. S. Lewis, *From Reflections on the Psalms* (N.p.: Harcourt, n.d.), 64.

## Week 8 · Day 5

*God is building you
as living stones
into His house.
His custom house.*

-JOHN BEVERE

God is the Master Builder. It is with great love and care that He constructs His house, Jesus being the foundation. In Christ we become temples of the Holy Spirit, vessels who are called and equipped for the Master's awe-inspiring eternal purposes. The Lord Himself dwells within us, His church. This was His plan and true desire, and we get to be forever blessed by it!

> For the LORD has chosen Zion; He has desired it for His dwelling place: "This is My resting place forever; here I will dwell, for I have desired it."
>
> -PSALM 132:13-14

We are not dead materials, but living stones, alive and part of God's plans.

> You also, as living stones, are being built up a spiritual house, a holy priesthood, to offer up spiritual sacrifices acceptable to God through Jesus Christ.
>
> -1 PETER 2:5

God is working in our lives as His building – molding us and shaping us – as part of His own home. And we also have a living, spiritual purpose within that home. Our spiritual sacrifice is obedience to His Word, a life made acceptable to God through Jesus. We become workers together with God. By His empowering grace, we have a job to do. Our lives take on new and eternal meaning!

God fashioned us by His own will. He didn't need us, but He made us and chose us as His own. He desired to dwell in us and to work with us in His great plan! You have been made for eternity, to play a part in God's ever-unfolding, ever-existing purposes.

**Being driven by eternity means you get to be a part of God's own beautiful custom home, and you have a rewarding job to do as part of the household of faith!**

Have you found your place in God's home? Are you seeking Him and finding your purpose there?

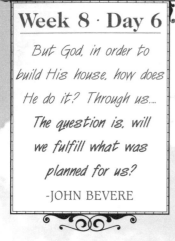

## Week 8 · Day 6

*But God, in order to build His house, how does He do it? Through us....*

*The question is, will we fulfill what was planned for us?*

-JOHN BEVERE

We are co-laborers with the Lord (1 Cor. 3:9). That means we have a role to play in His eternal plans. We have a part that God chose to give us of His own accord. We are of the household of faith, the family of God. You are created as God's own workmanship, and He wants you to do your part, carrying out the plans He has prepared for *you!*

> For we are God's workmanship, created in Christ Jesus to do good works, which God prepared in advance for us to do.
> -EPHESIANS 2:10, NIV

Understand that God prepared plans for you that He desires you to complete!

Whenever people work together in a family or as a team, if someone doesn't pull their own weight, either that job doesn't get done or someone else has to work harder to make up for it. There are people with whom God has called you to share His love. There are poor in the world whom the Lord desires for you to bless with your resources. At your job, you have the opportunity to be God's messenger, His hands and feet. Prisoners, widows, orphans, the sick, the unsaved – the needs are great, and so is the power inside you to do what God has called you to do as your part in His kingdom.

And of course, your church is one of the most important places God has prepared for you to be involved in, using your gifts and talents.

*Perhaps you've never realized it, but there are people and plans in the earth that depend on you!* You are important to God as His child and in His eternal purpose. He has called you from eternity past to walk in His ways according to His divine blueprint. **God's good works are prepared in advance and waiting for you!** Isn't it sobering to know that He will build His house with or without us?

## Week 8 · Day 7

*There's sovereignty;
God says, "I'll build my
house and it'll be finished,
it'll be done." But then
there's free will; God
says, "You have a choice.
You'll give an account of
what's in the past."
Every moment's been
laid out, but have you
fulfilled it?"*

-JOHN BEVERE

There are some who are called to be school teachers, accountants, or truck drivers, but they live their lives as pastors or ministers. Others are called to be evangelists, Bible college professors, or missionaries, but they live life as plumbers or business people. Some are called to be associates, but they spend a lifetime in the wrong position as the senior person in the organization.

When you stand before the Lord at the Judgment Seat of Christ, it is the role you were supposed to fulfill that you will be judged according to, not the role you chose for yourself. All works of self will be burned up; only the works that were of the Lord will remain and be rewarded.

Everyone has a call from God. Whether you are called to be a faithful homemaker, doorman, pastor, doctor, evangelist or Bible teacher, it is living in what God has called you to do that will bring you great rewards in heaven. Living in the wrong call will result in a life with few or no rewards in eternity.

**The first step to knowing and living in what God has called you to do is to seek Him, follow His ways, and ask Him to reveal His will to you for your life.** No one can do this for you, although, as you are involved in your local church, there will be those who can help steer you. You must seek Him in faith, diligently. It can be hard work, but it will reward you richly, now and in eternity. He may lead you at some times dramatically, but most times little by little, by His Word and Spirit. But rest assured, if you seek Him, He will lead and guide you. As you are faithful in the small things, He will bring you into greater clarity as He reveals His will for your life.

> But without faith it is impossible to please Him, for he who comes to God must believe that He is, and that He is a rewarder of those who diligently seek Him.
>
> -HEBREWS 11:6

It is a matter of faith. God does not tell you everything and do everything for you. As you daily pray and partake of His Word, He will make His ways known to you. You simply must ask, seek, and knock, and the door will be opened...the answers will come. Like Abraham and all others before you, you have to start out in faith, believing and following His Word in your daily living. He then leads you and guides you as you go, keeping your paths straight and choices sound as you obey Him.

What are the plans God has for you? Certainly He knows them and desires to share them with you so you can walk in His ways and please Him. Jeremiah gives us a glimpse into this.

> "For I know the plans I have for you," declares the LORD, "plans to prosper you and not to harm you, plans to give you hope and a future. Then you will call upon

me and come and pray to me, and I will listen to you. You will seek me and find me when you seek me with all your heart."

-JEREMIAH 29:11-13, NIV

God has great things for His people, full of hope and a blessed future. They are not always things we would have chosen or understood, but when we walk in His call, we are always thankful for His ways and blessed in the end. Many say they desire God's will, but His will is only made known to those who diligently seek Him with their whole heart. *Keeping a portion of your heart in the world while trying to seek God is like trying to swim with one leg in the water and one on shore.*

### *Driven by Eternity:*
## YOUR WEEK IN REVIEW

- Would your family, friends, and co-workers say you lived like a person driven by eternity?

- You will be judged according to what God has called you to do, not according to what you did.

- God chose us to cooperate with the Holy Spirit but He will build His house with or without us.

- Your work matters to God and to eternity.

- You are part of God's custom home, and you have a job to do in His household.

- Your job in God's kingdom has been prepared for you in advance by God Himself.

- God has given you the ability to know His ways and His will, but you have a choice.

God has plans for you, but do you feel you are you fulfilling them? Why or why not? What can you do to start fulfilling God's plans for your life?

_____

_____

Do you have "one leg in the water and one on shore," or are you seeking God with your whole heart and being?

_____

_____

O send out Your light and Your truth, let them lead me; let them bring me to Your holy hill and to Your dwelling.

-PSALM 43:3, AMP

*Father God, I desire to know Your will more fully in my life. I am excited to be a part of Your plans and purposes and to receive rewards one day in heaven. I am blessed to help others know You also.*

*I won't lean on my own understanding, but in all my ways I will acknowledge You. I ask You to direct my paths. Send out Your light and truth, and let them lead me, Lord! I desire to live a life driven by eternity, a life of prayer and obedience to Your Word. Help me in the small things, Lord; show me Your will as I seek You and obey in these daily. I turn the eyes of my understanding toward You, and my ears, so I may see and hear Your direction in the greater things as well.*

*Bring me to Your holy hill, Lord, to Your dwelling. In Your presence is fullness of joy. I ask You, Holy Spirit, to come into my heart in a fresh way as I seek and fulfill the life that God has for me.*

*In Jesus' name, amen.*

# God's Custom Home

Thus says the LORD: "Heaven is My throne, and earth is My footstool. Where is the house that you will build Me? And where is the place of My rest? For all those things My hand has made, and all those things exist," says the LORD.

-ISAIAH 66:1

"I'm God. What do you think you can do for Me? I own Heaven. As a matter of fact, I measured the entire universe with the span of My hand. I'm the one who put the stars in the universe with My fingers. I'm the one that weighed every drop of water in your planet with the palm of My hand. I'm God; do you really know who I am?" So He says, "What do you think you can do for Me?"

This is like a bunch of little ants walking up to you, saying, "We're going to build you a house." You go, "Oh, yeah, right. Like you're going to build me a house." That is absolutely vain. [But] that makes more sense than us saying, "God, we're going to do something for You."

-JOHN BEVERE

1. If our human ability to do something of eternal value for God is basically zero, how are we to serve Him or do anything for Him?

_____

_____

_____

The second part of Isaiah 66:2 gives some insight into the previous question:

But on this one will I look: On him who is poor and of a contrite spirit, and who trembles at My word.

2. What does this verse mean? Describe the type of person God is looking for.

_____

_____

_____

Look at John 15:5:

I am the vine, you are the branches. He who abides in Me, and I in him, bears much fruit; for without Me you can do nothing.

3. What is true biblical humility?

_____

_____

4. Can you think of two or three Scriptures, that show how God is able to empower His people for His service in the kingdom?

_____

_____

_____

5. Although we can do nothing for God in our own power, still He chose to include us in His eternal plans and purposes. This is truly amazing! What role does obedience have to play, and why is it so important?

_____

> We work together as partners who belong to God. You are God's field, God's building – not ours.
>
> -1 CORINTHIANS 3:9, NLT

6. That we are privileged to be called co-laborers with God is almost beyond our imagination. Did you ever realize that your assignment on earth was actually to be part of building God's house?

_____

_____

_____

**hot TOPIC** Have you ever experienced the thrill and deep satisfaction of cooperating with God? Have His Word and Spirit ever led you to be a co-laborer with Him and you saw the blessed results in your life or others? Perhaps you prayed for something or someone and it came to pass, or you gave your time or resources and saw results for God's kingdom. Maybe the Lord gave you a warning or a word about something important. Write the story.

_____

_____

**God wants you to have more of Himself!** How can you live each day to have more of these God-things happen in your life? (Think about what you do daily, your level of prayer and the Word, your involvement in your church and obedience to the Lord.)

_____

_____

God is the Master Builder, and we are His workmanship, His building material for His house. Jesus is the foundation of God's house. We are created in Christ for good works. As part of God's house we have a job to do, assignments from God for which we will be rewarded if we are obedient in what He has given us to do.

For no one can lay any foundation other than the one already laid, which is Jesus Christ. If any man builds on this foundation using gold, silver, costly stones, wood, hay or straw, his work will be shown for what it is, because the Day will bring it to light. It will be revealed with fire, and the fire will test the quality of each man's work. If what he has built survives, he will receive his reward. If it is burned up, he will suffer loss; he himself will be saved, but only as one escaping through the flames.

-1 CORINTHIANS 3:11-15, NIV

7. Have you been a wise builder and laid a sure foundation? Write some specific things, things that will survive the fires of the Judgment Seat of Christ, in which you have been obedient to the Lord, following Him from your heart, by the Holy Spirit. (Examples may be witnessing, giving, visiting the poor, prayer, etc.)

8. As you write these things, what is the Holy Spirit saying to you?

**The real question is, will we fulfill what He planned for us?** God had a plan for us before we were even born. He has works prepared in advance for us, from all eternity. If He has called us to be one thing, we must not choose another, or all we do will be in vain for eternity's rewards! We are rewarded according to our faithfulness to our calling from God, not according to what we do on our own.

- Think of King David, who started out as a young boy and went through all kinds of trials, even having attempts made on his life and living in caves at one point, before finally becoming king.
- Remember Joseph, who had dreams from God about leading his family and even nations, but first was sold by his own brothers, falsely accused, imprisoned, and forgotten. But ultimately His dreams came to pass.
- The apostle Paul went from a religious murderer to having his life supernaturally interrupted by God, going on to become an apostle of love, grace, and power.
- Don't forget Peter, who cursed and denied the Lord, but later became the apostle who would feed the Lord's sheep!

*All of these had adversity and even failings, but each was faithful to God's Word and Spirit as they fulfilled His will. You can do the same in what God has for you!*

## How are you doing so far?

9.  And now, how about you? How has your life shaped up so far? Can you see some parallels in your life with someone in the Bible? If so, who?

_____

_____

_____

10. As you have looked at these people from the Bible, what is God saying to you right now to encourage you, as He is working to bring you along His path for your life?

_____

_____

_____

## The future.

11. How is God preparing you to fulfill the plans He has?

_____

_____

_____

**ZENITH**
the time when something is most powerful or successful.

Winning and success are measured by God's standards, not our own or the world's. You've heard many life-altering truths in this session, and you have choices to make. If you will seek and follow the Lord, He will be found, and He will reveal Himself to you!

> But he who heard and did nothing is like a man who built a house on the earth without a foundation, against which the stream beat vehemently; and immediately it fell. And the ruin of that house was great.
>
> -LUKE 6:49

Let the Holy Spirit challenge you now; it's never too late. Do not be like the person who hears and does nothing. Be someone who builds on the foundation of Jesus, God's Word, and you will be able to withstand all the storms of the enemy, the lure of the flesh, and the onslaught of the world system!

What is the thing that most challenged you or blessed you in this session?

_____

_____

_____

_____

# God's Custom House Part 2

# HOUR 9

Please refer to Chapter 11,

God's Custom House,

in the *Driven by Eternity* book

and video session 9.

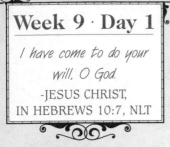

*I have come to do your will, O God.*

-JESUS CHRIST,
IN HEBREWS 10:7, NLT

It's less than ten words, but its message proves it to be one of the most meaningful sentences anywhere, anytime. Jesus came into the world as an infant, then a flame of fire burning brightly with an unparalleled sense of purpose. Eternity was His "middle name," His heartbeat, His creed. Eternity flowed from Him in all He did. Look at the power and poetry of this passage:

> Therefore, when He came into the world, He said: "Sacrifice and offering You did not desire, but a body You have prepared for Me. In burnt offerings and sacrifices for sin You had no pleasure. Then I said, 'Behold, I have come – in the volume of the book it is written of Me – to do Your will, O God.'"
>
> -HEBREWS 10:5-7

One hundred percent God, one hundred percent man from the very time He came into the world, Jesus made it known that He was all about accomplishing God's mission, doing the will of His Father. Obedience was what the Father wanted, and Jesus made it clear from the beginning that He would perfectly, willingly, and lovingly comply.

In obedience to His Father He chose to take on a human body and to give that life for our salvation, our eternal well-being.

There is a lot we can draw from this passage that applies to our call, too. Like Jesus, we have a body that we must dedicate and consecrate to God. We have decisions to make each moment of each day about whether or not we will de driven by eternity or driven by self, the world, or Satan.

Like Jesus we must understand that God desires our obedience in all things and that only in our obedience to God's calling, God's Word, and God's plans and purposes will we fulfill our destinies.

We too have a life that we must give to God. We too must obey God our Father. We too must sacrifice our own will and follow God's plans. Jesus is our example, and we must declare with Him, by the power of His Spirit, "Behold, I have come to do Your will, O Lord!"

Can you truly say today, "Behold, I have come to do Your will, O Lord"? If so, how are you accomplishing that in your life? If not, what do you need to do to be able to say that?

## Week 9 · Day 2

*Is it possible to change diapers to the glory of God? You bet, if that's where you belong. Is it possible to deliver mail to the glory of God? Certainly, if that's where God has called you. ...And if you know you are fulfilling the divine purpose intended for you at this season of your life, it's much easier to resist those enticing cries that try to seduce you away from your true calling. Knowing your divine purpose gives you a stability and strength that leads to victorious living.*

-DAVID JEREMIAH

Jesus came to save sinners, and only by God's grace, do they begin to see their sin, helplessness, and desperate need for a Savior. We must recognize our sin, flee from it into the arms of Christ, and be forgiven, born again with a new nature. We need to be filled with the Holy Spirit and live accordingly, obedient to God's Word. We must search and seek God for our purpose and place.

We also must be careful not to convey that God's plans will never involve suffering or sacrifice. On the contrary, God's will for each of us is all about giving up our ways and the world's ways to follow Christ. This does not mean that nothing will come against that purpose, for it is the objective of the enemy to entice us away from all God has ordained for us. But the knowledge of what we are called to do will keep us on the path to pleasing our Creator and entering into great reward in heaven and on earth.

Despite the hardships and suffering, Jesus had joy that no one can fathom, power we can hardly comprehend, and peace that all of us long for! He had power over all demons, was a healer and friend to the needy, and was a voice of ultimate authority. How did He do it? By the power of the Holy Spirit and by obediently following God's will in every circumstance.

We are not Jesus. But we are saved by His sacrifice, empowered by the same Holy Spirit, and we can fulfill our heavenly Father's will for our lives, just as Jesus did. We too can have great joy, peace, and the Spirit's power!

Therefore, whether you eat or drink, or whatever you do, do all to the glory of God.
-1 CORINTHIANS 10:31

If you will seek Him and obey Him, He will see to it that you have what you need and be placed where you need to be at the perfect timing. Just as it was for Jesus your Master.

Are you experiencing the joy, power, and peace that Jesus did – no matter what your circumstances? How can you do so?

_____

_____

_____

_____

_____

_____

1. David Jeremiah, *Prayer, the Great Adventure* (Sisters, OR: Multnomah, 2004), 212.

## Week 9 · Day 3

*There are people that are just floating right now. Or, they're just out there trying to earn a living. I find that about 85 percent to 90 percent of the people in America that attend church...listen to a sermon for an hour and go back out and basically do their thing for the rest of the week. They don't have that vision from heaven....Yet, God says, I will show every one of you what you're called to do.*

*-JOHN BEVERE*

There is more than one reason most people just "put in their time" when it comes to living life. Some go through the motions of living, appear content to eat, sleep, work and then do it again with little or no involvement in anything outside their own daily needs.

Many people do want to go beyond a mundane existence to a life that is filled with purpose and satisfaction, where there is abundant evidence of that success. Just look at the very large self-help, self-improvement, and New Age industries. Lots of people have questions about living with a sense of destiny.

Not all answers to this question are created equally. While there are many good principles taken from the business, educational, and religious worlds, there are also severe pitfalls. These lead to all sorts of unscriptural practices and often to people who are disappointed with the god they created, in an image far from biblical truth. All genuine truth, beauty, and knowledge come from God. **To find your answers go to the source, God's Word and Spirit.**

Call to me and I will answer you. I'll tell you marvelous and wondrous things that you could never figure out on your own.
    -JEREMIAH 33:3, THE MESSAGE

God has marvelous and wonderful things to tell you. For all in your life you could never figure out on your own, the Lord is there. Call to Him; He has promised He will answer you! Seek for that vision from heaven.

What insight have you received today about the answers to situations you may be facing?

_____

_____

_____

_____

_____

_____

_____

_____

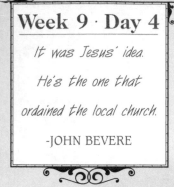

## Week 9 · Day 4

*It was Jesus' idea.*

*He's the one that*

*ordained the local church.*

-JOHN BEVERE

Never underestimate the impact you will have if you choose to be driven by eternity!

In the world, as you go about your daily affairs at work, home, and recreation, you have the opportunity to make a real difference. Think of all the friends, family, co-workers, and even acquaintances you can influence for the Lord.

Your family needs the gospel as much as the orphan in Russia – you can see to it that they get it. Your co-workers spend thousands of hours with you; surely you have opportunity to pray for them and bless them as the Lord leads you. The delivery person, the Fed-Ex or UPS driver you only see for a few moments can benefit from a kind word or some help with the packages. Perhaps they will come to salvation because of a book or CD you hand them with a gleam in your eye as you tell them how it changed your life or got you through your tough times.

There is another extremely powerful way we can make an eternal impact, your local church. The Lord has called you as an important part in this caring family of believers! Reach out and get involved. God has a church for you. In doing so, you will find personal enrichment you never imagined because God has ordained it to be so! In fact, it is in large part from this that we will find the strength to do all the things we've shared here. It is also one of the most joyous, fulfilling, and practical things God ever gave us!

Those who are planted in the house of the LORD shall flourish in the courts of our God.

-PSALM 92:13

Do you want to flourish? To feel a genuine part of something bigger than yourself? To be needed and to help those in need? Grab hold of this truth; make the decision, pray, and get involved in a Bible-believing church!

In the court of God at the judgment, if you have served God in your local church, you will find you have touched multitudes! And you will be rewarded for all of eternity!

What is God saying to you about your involvement in your church?

_____

_____

_____

_____

_____

_____

_____

_____

## Week 9 · Day 5

*How can you fulfill your destiny if you're not even in the right location? How can the palm tree fulfill its destiny if it's in Alaska? It can't fulfill its destiny. One of the main reasons people are not fulfilling their destiny is they are not planted in a local church.*

-JOHN BEVERE

Only if a seed is planted in the right place can it properly germinate, take root, grow, and bear fruit. It can be a great seed, but in the wrong place it will lie dormant, producing nothing, or it will die.

If you transplant a seed over and over you will eventually stunt it or ruin it. On the other hand, if you let it grow in good soil, when harsh conditions come, the roots will go deeper, making it stronger.

The same applies to us. God has the prescribed soil for us in which to grow – the right location, right group of believers, a church body He wants us to be a part of, lending our gifts, resources, and talents. As we do this, our roots grow deeper and deeper in Him. He sustains and blesses our life, causing us to bear more and more fruit as we flourish in Him. We are to worship together continually and regularly as a way of life, upholding one another, invigorating our faith, and celebrating our God. Through this we will grow and walk in our destiny.

Let's keep a firm grip on the promises that keep us going. He always keeps his word. Let's see how inventive we can be in encouraging love and helping out, not avoiding worshiping together as some do but spurring each other on, especially as we see the big Day approaching.

-HEBREWS 10:23-25, THE MESSAGE

We all at times feel small and insignificant, like a tiny seed. But God has great plans for that seed. What is the Holy Spirit saying to you about your skills and abilities – big and small – and how He wants to grow you as you serve Him in your church?

# Week 9 · Day 6

*We're talking about how to find out what the call of God is on your life. If I have a bunch of seeds in my hand, but I don't know what those seeds are, how do I find out what their destiny is? Plant them! Just put them in the dirt. And you know what? Their destiny will come forth.*

-JOHN BEVERE

Like a wise master gardener, God will plant us in His church, in a local body of believers, causing us to grow, bloom, and prosper if we will allow Him to. There is a great truth to be had in this if we will hear what the Spirit is saying to us. If you are unsure of your calling in life, plant yourself in the church. That seed of the unknown will begin to grow and bear fruit, and your destiny will be made known!

So many people worry and fret over who God made them to be, what God wants them to do, what is the essence and fullness of their God-given destiny. And God desires us to know those things. But as in all things of the kingdom, we must follow God's ways, which are very different from ours.

Remember the boy shepherd David. First he had to slay the lion, then the bear, and then he graduated to the giant Goliath. Only after many more experiences where he proved faithful to God did he finally walk in his high call as the mighty King David, the man after God's own heart.

Our local church is where we will slay the lion, the bear, and today's spiritual Goliaths as we submit to God's plan, serving with whatever abilities He has given us. As we serve God in the church, we will develop blessed relationships, we will receive help for our life, and we can give of our own life to assist others in need. And there is something else the Lord does that is remarkable. *In the local church setting we can experience the awesome power of collective worship, prayer, and combined resources!*

God will reach our world through each of us as we come together in localized bodies of believers, putting our talents and gifts together to answer the cries of a lost and hurting world. Now that is an inspiring destiny, and you must find your place in it! Plant yourself in good soil and watch as God reveals to you who you really are and what you should be doing. You will see fruit, and clarity of purpose will come!

Pray for yourself and the leaders and members of your church for purpose and destiny.

_____

_____

_____

_____

_____

_____

_____

## Week 9 · Day 7

There are three reasons people don't find their God-given call or their destiny. The first is they simply do not diligently seek the Lord to know it. The second reason is they don't get truly planted in a good local church. The third is they become entangled in the world.

Becoming entangled in the world means that things like money, security, and unhealthy relationships become the stuff of our life, the driving force behind our decisions, our intentions, or actions. We become driven by these instead of by things of eternal value.

Now, money and a level of security and healthy relationships can be good, but anything that is put out of priority becomes a snare when it comes to the things of eternity. As we go about our daily lives, we need to be on guard in our hearts and minds that these sensitive and important areas do not consume us or take us off track from serving God.

Years ago there was a popular term in the church. "Dying to self" was considered a priority, and anyone who made it their aim was counted among the most blessed and spiritual among us. All were encouraged to follow it as a course of life; crucifying the lusts of the flesh and not giving place to the devil were great truths and counted as part of serious discipleship.

You don't hear much of that today. Yet look at what Jesus said.

The truth is, a kernel of wheat must be planted in the soil. Unless it dies it will be alone – a single seed. But its death will produce many new kernels – a plentiful harvest of new lives. Those who love their life in this world will lose it. Those who despise their life in this world will keep it for eternal life.

-JOHN 12:24-25, NLT

We have talked a lot about seeds and our being planted in good soil and about growth and destiny. But today's society, while loving to hear about growth, flourishing and destiny, rarely likes to hear about sacrifice. The truth is, though, there is no way to fulfill the high calling God has given each of us if we refuse to be planted and buried, dead to our old worldly life. Only then does He raise us to new life.

To refuse this is to live alone, on our own, apart from God's destiny. But if we will be as dead persons to the world's system, we will multiply and produce a great harvest. When you reckon yourself dead to the world, you have really begun to conquer. Why? Because Satan or the flesh can't successfully tempt a "dead" man or woman with lust or covetousness. You can't make a "dead" man or woman afraid to witness about Jesus. And "dead" people don't fear persecution, poverty, or other things that the flesh, the world or Satan try to use to stop us. The person who is dead to the world, but alive in Christ, is the person who is truly free to fulfill a great destiny and to be rewarded for it!

The more fruit you produce, the more rewards you will receive. *Many are called; will you be one of the chosen?*

*Driven by Eternity:*
## YOUR WEEK IN REVIEW

- Can you, like Jesus, say, "I have come to do Your will, O Lord"?

- Whatever you do, do it for the Lord, and He will take care of you.

- The answers to life are found in God's Word as He enlightens us by His Spirit.

- At the judgment, if you have served God in your local church, you will find you have touched multitudes.

- As we worship together in our local church, we grow and walk in our destiny.

- If you are unsure of your calling, plant yourself in the church. As that seed begins to grow and bear fruit, your destiny will be made known!

- Many are called but few chosen. To receive your reward, you must not be entangled with the world.

**Thank God for His precious Word and Holy Spirit!**

Call to me and I will answer you. I'll tell you marvelous and wondrous things that you could never figure out on your own.

-JEREMIAH 33:3, THE MESSAGE

There are three simple keys to know and fulfill your destiny. Pray about them individually, and then write what God is saying to you about each. *You will be blessed greatly if you take some time to do this and obey the Lord as He tells you things you could never figure out on your own.*

1. You must seek God diligently.

_____

_____

2. You must be planted in a local church.

_____

_____

3. You must not be entangled in the things of the world.

*Every one of us is going to touch people's lives if we just do what we're called to do,*
*even though we may not see the ripple effects of it here in this earth.*
*-JOHN BEVERE*

---

## THE THREE KEYS TO DESTINY

**ONE: You must diligently seek the Lord.**

Every single human being has a call on his or her life. You have a divine call. Nobody else has been given the assignment you've been given. But how do we know our calling? **The first step to knowing and fulfilling God's destiny for you is to seek Him diligently, asking Him to reveal His will to you for your life.** No one can do this for you, although the Lord can send godly people, good books, and things of this sort to assist you. This will take discipline; however, it brings the richest of rewards now and in eternity.

Be cautious not to expect God to always speak to you or lead you in dramatic ways. He may or may not, but it is His choice, not yours. *He will most often reveal things to you little by little by His Word and Spirit as you serve.* As you are faithful in little things, He will promote you to more for His glory.

> Ask, and it will be given to you; seek, and you will find; knock, and it will be opened to you. For everyone who asks receives, and he who seeks finds, and to him who knocks it will be opened. Or what man is there among you who, if his son asks for bread, will give him a stone? Or if he asks for a fish, will he give him a serpent? If you then, being evil, know how to give good gifts to your children, how much more will your Father who is in heaven give good things to those who ask Him!
>
> -MATTHEW 7:7-11

Jesus poses a great question here. If a person, even with an evil nature, would not betray the confidence of his children but would give them their food to eat, how much more will God our loving, heavenly Father care for us? Rest assured that if you seek Him, He will lead and guide you.

1.  In your occupation and also your church, what would you say God has called you to be doing, and how are you going about it as of right now?

    _____

    _____

2. What do you see for the future?

3. Right now, do you feel you are where you should be in life, according to God's will? Why or why not?

4. When was the last time you really sought God about all the above?

5. What was the result, and how did you follow through on it?

*In life, there is what you are doing and what you should be doing.* It is your responsibility to find God's call for your life. You alone will stand before Him one day and give an account for your time on earth. So take a good, objective look at your life.

6. Does it bear the signs of someone who diligently seeks God for His will? If so, how exactly does your life prove this?

But without faith it is impossible to please Him, for he who comes to God must believe that He is, and that He is a rewarder of those who diligently seek Him.

-HEBREWS 11:6

Seeking God's will is a matter of faith. God does not tell you everything, nor does He do everything for you. As you daily pray, study His Word, and follow Him, He will make more of His ways known to you. Like Abraham and all others before you, you have to start out in faith, believing and following His Word in your daily living. He then leads you and guides you as you go, setting your paths straight as you obey Him.

Can you write about some things in your life that show you have made choices to follow the Lord as you knew best, and He met you at that place in your life and then revealed more?

## TWO: You must be planted in the house of God.

Those who are planted in the house of the LORD shall flourish in the courts of our God.

-PSALM 92:13

The church is made up of believers all around the globe. The local church could be described as a specific group of believers who identify with a local community. These continually and regularly gather together in fellowship and communion to worship, pray, and celebrate God. They also learn of God (doctrine) and serve the Lord and each other as well as intentionally reaching out to the world.

7. Whose idea was the local church?

8. Who is it that builds the church?

9. How does the church get built if the builder is not physically present?

10. What do "the courts of our God" refer to in Psalm 92:13?

11. Why is this important to you as far as your relationship to the local church?

12. What does 1 Corinthians 12:18 have to do with you choosing what church to be a part of?

> But now God has set the members, each one of them, in the body just as He pleased.
>
> -1 CORINTHIANS 12:18

_____

_____

_____

13. What happens to the church when we are not properly functioning in it?

_____

_____

_____

**The beauty of being planted: A miracle takes place!** One of the great secrets or keys to finding your destiny is to plant yourself in the local church.

> He shall be like a tree planted by the rivers of water, that brings forth its fruit in its season, whose leaf also shall not wither; and whatever he does shall prosper.
>
> -PSALM 1:3

Even if you have little or no idea what you could do or offer or what God's will for you is, _that is all the more reason to get involved._ Here's why: Think of the biblical seed analogy. Even if a person hasn't a clue as to what seeds he has to plant, once they are planted and begin to grow, you will soon see exactly what their type and purpose is! _As the plant comes to fruition, identity and destiny are revealed!_

Every one of us has a calling in the local church. We are not to be fragmented or doing our own thing, but rather we are to plug into what God is doing. We do this by coming into meaningful relationship with those in our local church, not just visiting and then leaving. You must find your place and humbly serve. The church grows, not solely because of the pastor or leaders, but because all members submit to God's authority, find their place, and function in unity together!

> Under his direction, the whole body is fitted together perfectly. As each part does its own special work, it helps the other parts grow, so that the whole body is healthy and growing and full of love.
>
> -EPHESIANS 4:16, NLT

Some people are naturally "volunteer" types or "people persons," and they have no trouble joining a group and becoming quickly plugged in. _You are not just a volunteer; you are a servant with a destiny, called by God and empowered with His grace by the Holy Spirit and His Word._

14. What is the Lord saying to you here, now? How does that statement change your heart and attitude toward serving in the local church and fulfilling your destiny?

_____

_____

_____

15. Does it cause you to want to take action? Remember what happens to a plant if it is transplanted every couple months – the root system dwarfs and eventually stops bearing fruit or even dies. You need to be in the right church, according to God's will, not your own, planted firmly and flourishing.

_____

_____

_____

16. What do you need to do about this specific key to your destiny?

_____

_____

_____

## THREE: You must not become entangled with the world.

_And he said to them all_, If any man will come after me, let him deny himself, and take up his cross daily, and follow me. For whosoever will save his life shall lose it: but whosoever will lose his life for my sake, the same shall save it.
-LUKE 9:23-24, EMPHASIS ADDED

You need not fear that if you follow Jesus you will end up less blessed or fulfilled than if you go your own way. Don't be fooled by illusions either. The fact is, among the very few who make it to the "top" of society, there are plenty of bitter, sad people. There are daily accounts of movie stars, pop music and sports stars, business moguls, and other hugely "successful" men and women who are or were miserable, unfulfilled, lonely, and even suicidal. And don't forget, sinners live like sinners; that's what sinners do. _Only in being the person God made us to be will we ever find true joy, peace, and contentment._

Examine yourselves as to whether you are in the faith. Test yourselves. Do you not know yourselves, that Jesus Christ is in you? – unless indeed you are disqualified.
-2 CORINTHIANS 13:5

But none of these things move me; _nor do I count my life dear to myself, so that I may finish my race with joy_, and the ministry which I received from the Lord Jesus, to testify to the gospel of the grace of God.
-ACTS 20:24, EMPHASIS ADDED

I do all this to spread the Good News, and *in doing so I enjoy its blessings.* Remember that in a race everyone runs, but only one person gets the prize. You also must run in such a way that you will win. All athletes practice strict self-control. They do it to win a prize that will fade away, but we *do it for an eternal prize. So I run straight to the goal with purpose in every step.* I am not like a boxer who misses his punches. I discipline my body like an athlete, training it to do what it should.

-1 CORINTHIANS 9:23-27, NLT, EMPHASIS ADDED

God wants you to be really blessed! So ask yourself some penetrating questions.

17. Are you entangled with the world? Do you count your life dear to yourself, first loving yourself and your "stuff," or do you run with God's purpose in your every step?

_____

_____

_____

_____

18. Do you obey God's Word and the Holy Spirit no matter the circumstance, or do you rationalize faith away?

_____

_____

_____

_____

**ZENITH**
the time when something is most powerful or successful.

What is the Lord saying to you? What is the most important thing you have taken away from this hour that will cause you to be one who fulfills your destiny and is rewarded in heaven?

_____

_____

_____

_____

_____

_____

_____

_____

_____

_____

_____

_____

# Multiplication Part 1

## HOUR 10

Please refer to Chapter 12,

Multiplication,

in the *Driven by Eternity* book

and video session 10.

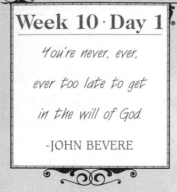

## Week 10 · Day 1

*You're never, ever, ever too late to get in the will of God.*

-JOHN BEVERE

Nothing really surprises God. He knows your beginning, end, and everything in between. When you foul up, make a mistake, or even sin, God has seen it already. He has also seen if you have a repentant heart and life. And He still, of course, has His plan for you!

Isaiah 66:2 says the one God esteems is the one who is poor and of a contrite spirit and trembles at His Word. The word *contrite* means "quick to repent" as well as "broken." A wild horse that is broken is not a horse that is ruined. Just the opposite! It is one that has all that energy, all that glory, fire, beauty, and strength reined in and ready to obey even the slightest command from its rider. That horse can become a champion!

Don't look at repentance from an Old Testament perspective of beating yourself up and wearing sackcloth and ashes. Repentance really means a complete change of mind or heart. *You lived and viewed things a certain way, and then the truth and wisdom of God come. As a result, you then say, "I'm letting go of my view, and I'm embracing the wisdom of God."* That's repentance.

You can do it with a lot of tears or with no tears, but either way it is born from your heart. It is when you truly say, "I am rejecting my view and embracing the wisdom of God." This kind of repentance is the authentic kind that is born of the grace of God; it will yield the peaceable fruits of righteousness. This repentance brings with it a life of holy obedience and growth in God, a life that is truly changed and that will impact eternity.

God's grace brings the change and strength needed to live according to His ways. And with that you are on track like the champion racehorse that can run and win for God's glory!

**It's never too late to get in the will of God!** Is there anything hindering you from being on track with God?

# Week 10 · Day 2

*For I am the least of the apostles, who am not worthy to be called an apostle, because I persecuted the church of God. But by the grace of God I am what I am, and His grace toward me was not in vain; but I labored more abundantly than they all, yet not I, but the grace of God which was with me.*

-THE APOSTLE PAUL,
IN 1 CORINTHIANS
15:9-10

Those are the words of the apostle Paul, about ten years before he was killed for his faith. By this time he had seen and been the instrument of countless miracles, taken three major apostolic journeys, set up more churches than anyone else in the world, had churches in Eastern Europe as well as all over Asia, yet he writes and says, *"I am the least of the apostles."* What *was* he thinking?

This is the Word of God, not a word of false humility. It is not something spoken by someone who actually was thinking in his heart how great he was. So why would Paul say this, in view of his great achievements? He says, "I've labored more than all of them, but I know it's the grace of God in me."

Paul was able to separate self from the grace of God. *We must realize there is nothing that we can do of eternal value apart from God giving us the ability to do it.* This kept Paul continually humble. When it came to working for the Lord, Paul understood the balance between himself and God's grace.

There's no boasting except in the Lord. He is the one who gives us the air we breathe, the life we have, and every ability and talent we possess. The people who accomplish the most for the Lord as they fulfill their destiny are the very people who understand this the most. The greatest among us is the servant of all. What a different worldview that is!

There is no room for evil pride in God's kingdom. It is one of the things He hates. *Where is your heart on this issue?* What is the root of your ambition? Do you want to achieve for your glory and enrichment, or for God's glory?

## Week 10 · Day 3

*Do you realize that God has a calling on your life, and the only thing you can do is mess it up? When you really figure that out, it totally liberates you from pride. All of a sudden you realize, "I can't improve on what He's called me to do. All I can do is mess it up." That revelation liberated me...I realized it was all about Him and not about me. All I have to do is be an obedient servant....Be bold in your obedience, but be an obedient servant.*

-JOHN BEVERE

ach of us has a different call from God, and we've been given the grace and abilities to fulfill it. Whether that calling is to lead or follow, be well-known or behind the scenes, we all are equally valuable and important in God's eyes.

Whether you are a best-selling author or the one who types the 150 bulletins for your Sunday school, if you are in God's will, you are right where you should be! What a relief! What a blessing! It makes no difference in the kingdom **as long as it is the place God has set you.** In God's army each is in perfect order, not breaking rank or stepping out of sequence. Envy and pride are lost in the heat of the battle and in the thrill of knowing who God really made you to be. In that knowledge contentment is found, and the kingdom flourishes as you serve. There is no need to fall into the sin of comparing ourselves one with another. We must compare ourselves to the call God has given us.

At the judgment, *titles, prosperity, and fame will be meaningless, but faithfulness to God is invaluable!*

Do you feel you have hindered God's calling on your life?

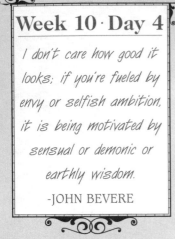

## Week 10 · Day 4

*I don't care how good it looks; if you're fueled by envy or selfish ambition, it is being motivated by sensual or demonic or earthly wisdom.*

-JOHN BEVERE

The degree to which we will fulfill God's plan for our lives will depend on the wisdom we operate in. Proverbs 24:3 says, "Through wisdom a house is built."

The Bible tells us that there are two wisdoms. We are building every moment of our lives – but the question is: With what wisdom are we building?

James 3:13-16 shows there's wisdom from heaven and there's wisdom which is not:

Who is wise and understanding among you? Let him show by good conduct that his works are done in meekness of wisdom. But if you have bitter envy and self-seeking [NIV, "selfish ambition"] in your hearts, do not boast and lie against the truth. This wisdom does not descend from above, but is earthly, sensual, demonic. For where envy and self-seeking exist, confusion and every evil thing are there.

That statement should put the healthy fear of God in each of us! No one wants "confusion and every evil thing" in their life! The point is, no matter what people do or how good it appears, if it's fueled by envy or selfish ambition, we are building with fleshly, sensual, or demonic motives.

W. E. Vines' dictionary defines *envy* as "the feeling of displeasure produced by witnessing or hearing of the advantage or prosperity of others." When you see somebody prosper around you, do you rejoice? Or do you feel, "How come that's not me?" Another definition is "the painful, resentful awareness of an advantage enjoyed by another, joined with a desire to possess the same advantage." Sounds pretty ugly when you put it in these very real terms, doesn't it?

If we view the call of God through the world's eyes, then envy is unavoidable. We must look at it through kingdom eyes. Paul writes about it in Philippians 1:15-17 (NIV): "It is true that some preach Christ out of envy and rivalry, but others out of good will. The latter do so knowing that I am put here for the defense of the Gospel. The former preach Christ out of selfish ambition."

There were some who envied Paul's success. They didn't understand that every one of us is given different callings. Everyone is given different graces to fulfill those callings. *If you start comparing yourself with somebody else in the body of Christ, you will begin to envy.* Don't be fooled; you can always point to some who have "more" than you, and of course, if you look around, there are always some who have "less" than you. Keep your eyes on God. The only person you're competing against is yourself. Envying others will cause discontent with God's call for your life.

How do you react when you see others prosper? Is envy bringing confusion and worse to your life? Talk to God, and let Him work out any envy from your heart today.

## Week 10 · Day 5

*Ambition is an eager and a strong desire to accomplish something. So, selfish ambition means you have an eager desire to accomplish something for your interest. Godly wisdom, on the other hand, will fuel kingdom passion, not selfish ambition.*

-JOHN BEVERE

The wisdom of God is pure. There is no hypocrisy in it. When you live in God's wisdom, there is no outward appearance of godliness mixed with envious or selfish motives burning on the inside of you. You wouldn't say to someone, "I'm so happy for you," while on the inside you're feeling, *I can't believe they got that success.*

> But the wisdom that is from above is first pure, then peaceable, gentle, willing to yield, full of mercy and good fruits, without partiality and without hypocrisy. Now, the fruit of righteousness is sown in peace by those who make peace.
>
> -JAMES 3:17-18

When you repent in humility of selfish ambition, God's grace can remove the fuel that causes you to act that way. When you declare, "God, it's my fault; I'm the one that has the problem here. Lord, I hate it, and I repent of it," God says, "I can take it out." And then He gives you grace to walk in His wisdom and freedom.

The goal is not to be the greatest, but to be obedient to your call. Many people, businesses, churches, and other organizations have failed because their goal was to be the biggest. But the army of God is to be a faceless army. In other words, they will not covet other's positions.

Godly wisdom rejoices at the advancement of God's kingdom whether it occurs through us or another. Remember John the Baptist said, "I must decrease that He may increase." He rejoiced when Jesus increased.

Godly wisdom is "willing to yield." The New International Version says it is "submissive." Godly wisdom is content in its call; therefore, it is willing and happily submitted to authority, especially God's delegated authority. It sees the big picture. **People who are submitted to godly authority are not selfishly ambitious. They walk in godly wisdom and are among those to be most greatly rewarded.**

What's inside of you? Envy and selfish ambition? Or peace, a submissive servant's heart, and godly wisdom? Let the Holy Spirit help you sort this question out.

## Week 10 · Day 6

*God delights in showing us exciting new alternatives for the future. Perhaps as you enter into a listening silence the joyful impression to learn how to weave or how to make pottery emerges. Does that sound too earthy, too unspiritual a goal? God is intently interested in such matters. Are you? Maybe you will want to learn and experience more about the spiritual gifts of miracles, healing, and tongues. Or you may do as one of my friends: spend large periods of time experiencing the gift of helps, learning to be a servant. Perhaps this next year you would like to read all the writings of C. S. Lewis, or D. Elton Trueblood. Maybe five years from now you would like to be qualified to work with handicapped children.'*

*-RICHARD J. FOSTER*

I nvesting quiet time with God will always reap eternal rewards. To be driven by eternity is to be driven to prayer. Jesus constantly went to prayer, and when He emerged, He impacted whole communities and ultimately all heaven and earth!

Taking quality time to make sure you are in God's will, to reevaluate your ambitions and goals, to make sure they are from God and not self, and then re-orienting your life as necessary are things we must regularly be doing. And remember, God speaks as much in the still, small voice as in the thunder and lightning. He may lead you to read God's Word to those in nursing homes, to study classical piano, or to be a blessing in a national ministry. Let Him decide. As you are obedient, He will bring it to pass and you will be blessed.

Seeking God's direction for your life, meditating in His Word, and listening to His Spirit bring focus where it belongs: on *God* and what He has called *you* to do, and not on comparing yourself with your own standards or with everybody else. Focusing on God's will for your life naturally results in blessings to others as God opens doors of opportunity to serve.

So concentrate on what God wants *you* to be doing, and use His Word and calling for your standard of measurement. Invest some quality time now. Reevaluate these things in your life today, listening to the Holy Spirit, and journaling God's direction.

1. Richard Foster, *Celebration of Discipline* (San Francisco: Harper SanFrancisco, 1998), 108.

# Week 10 · Day 7

*This is why every believer should spend quality time with God. They should pray, they should read Scripture, they should listen to anointed tapes and books, and they should attend church. As we do this, grace is multiplied in our life, giving us the ability to do more. I've seen this in all areas of my life....As I've grown in the Word of God, I've had the ability to do more in less time. You know what it's like? If I have a dull ax and I try to chop down a tree, it may take me all day to chop down that tree with that dull ax, but if I sharpen that ax, I can exert the same amount of energy and chop down five trees.*

-JOHN BEVERE

God has great things for His people! And sometimes we make it too difficult. If we will simply trust and obey the Lord daily in the "little" things, He will build on those and we will find we are living a life driven by eternity, a life that will one day at the judgment reap a great reward!

> His lord said to him, "Well done, good and faithful servant; you were faithful over a few things, I will make you ruler over many things. Enter into the joy of your lord."
>
> -MATTHEW 25:21

It sounds so simple that we tend not to believe it. We say, "This is God we're talking about; it must be complex!" But while it is true that God is vast and far beyond all comprehension, it is also true that He has revealed Himself to us as a loving heavenly Father, and He has made the gospel simple! *You can do this!* You can live this abundant life!

Take what you have and be faithful in that. Be wise in your life. Don't use your own standards or compare with others; don't boast about anything you have or have done – it is all a gift of God anyway! Second Corinthians 10:12 says, "For we dare not class ourselves or compare ourselves with those who commend themselves. But they, measuring themselves by themselves, and comparing themselves among themselves, are not wise."

And then in 1 Corinthians 4:7, in *The Message*, says, "Isn't everything you have and everything you are sheer gifts from God? So what's the point of all this comparing and competing?"

There is no point in comparing or competing with others. Start with what you have and yield it to God; then watch what happens. *All you've been given is by grace, and grace can be multiplied in your life*, as the apostle Peter states in 2 Peter 1:2. You can take the foundational things God has given you and multiply as you grow in obedience and intimate knowledge of the Lord. The more you do this, the more grace you can walk in, and that gives you the ability to do even more.

Grace and peace, when multiplied by getting in God's Word and becoming intimate with God, sharpen you. It is geometric. *As you build faithfulness, you build godly momentum!* The more you pray, the more you will pray. The more you obey, the easier it gets to obey. The more you get to know God, the more effective prayers become, the more effective meditating in the Word becomes, the more effective in reaching people and ministering to people you become. Why? *Because grace is being multiplied.* Doesn't that make you want to just dive in and serve God?

### *Driven by Eternity:*
## YOUR WEEK IN REVIEW

- It's never too late to get in the will of God!

- There is nothing that we can do of eternal value apart from God giving us the ability to do it.

- Titles, prosperity, and fame will be meaningless, but faithfulness to God's call is everything!

- Comparing yourself with others in the body of Christ causes the sin of envy.

- People that are submitted to godly authority are not selfishly ambitious.

- Seeking God's direction for your life, meditating on His Word, and listening to His Spirit bring focus where it belongs: on *God* and what He has called *you* to do.

- As you build faithfulness, grace is multiplied to you and you build godly momentum!

For today's prayer and journaling time, do two things: First, prayerfully write what God has most impressed upon you from this hour's devotions.

---

Second, do you tend to make your walk with God into something that's too hard or too legalistic? Is there no joy in it, or could there be lots more? God is in control, not you, and He desires a joyful, loving relationship, not a rigid set of rules and regulations. When we are truly in love with God, our obedience just flows and His grace is lavished upon us more and more! Let the Lord minister the freedom of that truth to you today!

# Driven by Eternity: Multiplication

### The parable of the talents

For the kingdom of heaven is like a man traveling to a far country, who called his own servants and delivered his goods to them. And to one he gave five talents, to another two, and to another one, to each according to his own ability; and immediately he went on a journey.

-MATTHEW 25:14-15

1. The parable can be found in its entirety in Mathew 25. What is the main emphasis of this parable?

2. What does this mean for the different ministries God has placed in the earth?

3. First Corinthians 4:7 says, "For who makes you differ from another? And what do you have that you did not receive?" What does that verse mean for you personally?

In the parable of the talents, every servant is given something. Every one has a call with abilities and talents that will accompany that call. Also, there are levels that are given according to each person's ability.

4. How does this play into whether or not you will hear "well done" at the judgment?

5. Although all you have is from God and you can't add to your calling or your gifts, what can you do to increase what God has given you?

> ## hot TOPIC
> Why might someone bury their talents?
>
> _____
> _____
> _____
> _____

6. God never gives an insignificant talent. Have you ever struggled with your feelings about your gifts and talents and how to use and multiply them?

   _____
   _____
   _____

7. Have you ever felt you were using your talents in the wrong place or ways?

   _____
   _____
   _____

8. What would the Lord say to minister life to you about your gifts and talents? Think in terms of some Scriptures that show God at work in your life. Here is one to get you started as the Holy Spirit speaks to you: "The Lord will perfect that which concerns me; Your mercy and loving-kindness, O Lord, endure forever" (Ps. 138:8, AMP).

   _____
   _____
   _____

9. What are you doing in your life, job, church, and family to multiply your talents? How is the Lord working in these?

   _____
   _____
   _____

10. The person given two and the person given five each increased their talents and were commended by the Lord with the very same words of praise. They were made rulers over many things in heaven. What was the said of the person who was unfaithful?

   _____
   _____
   _____
   _____

## The parable of the ten minas

Therefore He said: "A certain nobleman went into a far country to receive for himself a kingdom and to return. So he called ten of his servants, delivered to them ten minas, and said to them, 'Do business till I come.' But his citizens hated him, and sent a delegation after him, saying, 'We will not have this man to reign over us.' And so it was that when he returned, having received the kingdom, he then commanded these servants, to whom he had given the money, to be called to him, that he might know how much every man had gained by trading."

-LUKE 19:12-15

11. This parable can be found in its entirety in Luke 19. What do the minas represent?

_____

_____

_____

12. What is the critical relationship between how we multiply what is given us and our eternal rewards?

_____

_____

_____

13. In the parable of the talents, each was given differing gifts and abilities. What is the key difference between that and the parable of the minas?

_____

_____

_____

14. You can't add to what God gives you. But talk about 2 Peter 1:2. How can "grace and peace" be "multiplied to you"?

_____

_____

_____

15. What amazing and exciting thing happens when grace and peace are multiplied to you?

_____

_____

_____

**ZENITH**

the time when something is most powerful or successful.

**Your time on this earth can be multiplied. And do you want more rewards? Here's how!**

*It's so great how this happens!* The more you get to know God, the more effective prayer, meditating in the Word, reaching out and ministering to people become. Grace and wisdom are being multiplied, so you can do more. It becomes exponential, growing ever more as God builds on the foundation! His wisdom causes you to be able to do more in a day. You can think more effectively, pray and work more effectively, doing life's business more effectively.

How does it work, exactly? Check *this* out:

> But this I say: He who sows sparingly will also reap sparingly, and he who sows bountifully will also reap bountifully. So let each one give as he purposes in his heart, not grudgingly or of necessity; for God loves a cheerful giver. And God is able to make all grace abound toward you, that you, always having all sufficiency in all things, may have an abundance for every good work....Now may He who supplies seed to the sower, and bread for food, supply and multiply the seed you have sown and increase the fruits of your righteousness.
> -2 CORINTHIANS 9:6-8, 10

Don't miss it: Just like the parables of the talents and the minas, this verse goes far beyond money. If you give of your life to the Lord sparingly, you will reap sparingly. Who wants that? *If you sow your time, gifts, prayers, and abilities bountifully into God's kingdom, you will see them multiply – just like seeds sown in the field – into an ever growing and eternal harvest!* Watch how it multiplies over and over for you in amazing promises:

- God loves the cheerful giver! What could be better than His love?
- The more you plant, the more you reap.
- God is able to make all grace abound toward you so that you always have an abundance for every good work.
- You never run out, because He who supplies your seed multiplies it, giving you more seed to sow.

This continues over and over on into eternity! So what is stopping you from tearing down the walls that keep you from going for God 100 percent? He wants to multiply your life! What might be God's "power statement" to you right now as you see His principle of godly multiplication?

_____

_____

_____

_____

_____

_____

# Multiplication Part 2

## HOUR 11

Please refer to Chapter 12,

Multiplication,

in the *Driven by Eternity* book

and video session 11.

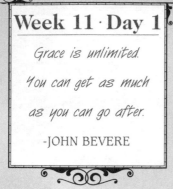

# Week 11 · Day 1

*Grace is unlimited.*

*You can get as much*

*as you can go after.*

-JOHN BEVERE

The apostle James wrote in his epistle, "But He gives more grace. Therefore He says: "God resists the proud, but gives grace to the humble" (James 4:6).

There are a lot of things in life that may offer you resistance, but it is a sure thing that the last thing you want is to be resisted by God!

Everything you have is from God. So there is absolutely no reason anyone could boast or be prideful in His presence or in life in general. In fact, pride is a sure way to get nowhere with God or in life.

We are not talking about taking a sense of achievement in a job well done or the warm feelings parents get when beholding their children. We are talking about the type of pride that causes you to be puffed up, thinking more highly of yourself than you should, thinking you're better than others, you have made success on your own, or you need nothing more than yourself.

Romans 12:3 has this to say to each one of us:

For I say, through the grace given to me, to everyone who is among you, not to think of himself more highly than he ought to think, but to think soberly, as God has dealt to each one a measure of faith.

Humility, though, goes hand in hand with grace. Now humility is not to be confused with being weak or lacking courage. King David declared "The Lord is the strength of my life! Whom shall I fear? What can man do to me?" Humility actually strengthens and protects you, keeping you sensitive to the heart of God so He can reveal His ways. And it empowers you to complete the calling God has on your life, as it brings more grace with it.

Psalm 25:9 shows that God leads the humble in what is right, teaching them His way. True humility is when we know we can't do anything apart from Him. It is demonstrated when we cooperate with God out of obedience. Since we are saved by grace, sustained by grace, and empowered to serve by grace, shouldn't we want as much as we can get?

**God gives grace to the humble, and He is calling you to go for more grace in your life.** How? By humbly seeking and following Him to know His Word and Holy Spirit intimately! How exciting, to always be able to get more of such a great gift!

How are you going after all the grace you can get, living humbly before God?

_____

_____

_____

_____

_____

_____

_____

*Now, there are several areas that we can multiply the grace of God in...One of the first is we can multiply through giving.*

-JOHN BEVERE

"God is love." Those words can be wonderful, depending on how they are used. It must not be an excuse to justify sin or weaken the character of God. "God is love, and He loves whatever I do" is poor theology. No, God doesn't love everything and anything we do. He loves righteousness and mercy. He loves His Word and when we obey it. God loves it when we are doing what He has called us to do. He loves us indeed in spite of our many failings, but that is not an excuse for a free lifestyle, molding God into our own image to satiate our desires.

God's love was shown to us clearly and profoundly when He gave the extravagant gift of Jesus. God gave the ultimate love sacrifice for a specific purpose. He did the same when He sent the Holy Spirit. In fact, everything God does is born from love and always with purpose. And that's how it should be with us, too.

Jesus was "the firstborn among many" and was given like an amazingly fruitful seed planted for all of humanity. Together Jesus and the Holy Spirit have multiplied fruit beyond our imagination. As we follow God's Word and example, giving out of love, sacrifice, and with purpose, God multiplies our gifts as well.

> And [God] Who provides seed for the sower and bread for eating will also provide and multiply your [resources for] sowing and increase the fruits of your righteousness [which manifests itself in active goodness, kindness, and charity].
>
> -2 CORINTHIANS 9:10, AMP

God loves a cheerful giver. Why? Because a cheerful giver is one who understands the ways of the kingdom. When God gave Jesus, though He experienced terrible pain and suffering, still God gave with joy because He was able to look beyond the sacrifice and see the harvest. That harvest is you along with all believers, and all good things that come from the Father! Multiplied infinitely and eternally, the fruit is still growing daily in countless ways.

The same type of thing happens when we give out of love, with joy, and with purpose. We see the harvest, the multiplication of our seed. Time, money, abilities, and talents – all we give to the Lord in faith is multiplied and will reap an eternal reward!

Think for a moment like an expert farmer for God. The more seeds you sow, the more you will reap. You can't out give God; He is an extravagant generous giver. Are you planting? Picture vast fields full of seed and harvest.

Have you given God something to work with, plenty of seeds He can multiply on your behalf and for others?

_____

_____

_____

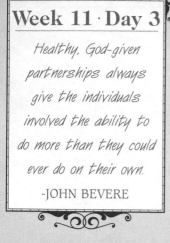

*Healthy, God-given partnerships always give the individuals involved the ability to do more than they could ever do on their own.*

-JOHN BEVERE

"Many hands make light work" is a great adage. If you have ever had to take on a large project, you know how great it is when others pitch in to help. All of a sudden, it's not such a daunting task. You are energized, and what would have taken much time, or maybe never been done, suddenly is in progress and then completed.

Going it alone is tough business. Any single mom knows how hard it is to be a team of one. Who watches the kids when they have to be home from school with a cold but Mom has to go to work?

When you are part of a good, local body of believers, help is on the way! The Lord always has willing, joyful servants who know their purpose. When it comes time to partner with God and His people they offer assistance, love, and more as needed. Thank God we have the Holy Spirit and the Word. We are NOT alone! And thank God for the church!

On a larger scale, nearly anything is within reach when individuals or groups join together in relationship. Cooperating together, sharing responsibility, setting and achieving their goals become almost miraculous as the power of unity, purpose, and God's calling drives them!

> I thank my God every time I remember you. In all my prayers for all of you, I always pray with joy *because of your partnership in the gospel* from the first day until now.
>
> -PHILIPPIANS 1:3-5, NIV, EMPHASIS ADDED

The apostle Paul was so impressed with the power of joining together in partnership that he said he thanked God *every time* he prayed for those who partnered with him for the gospel. And he said he prayed with *joy* because of it. This is because of the awesome power of our combined efforts!

Do you want to be the person who's responsible for people being filled with joy and see your own life blessed with joy and satisfaction? Start partnering with God's people and His ministries. Give your gifts, time, and abilities to goals that need your helping hand. You will see your gifts of time, money, and talents multiplied when you join God's team to reach the world with the gospel!

Can you see the power of a partnership? What is God showing you about this principle in your life?

_____

_____

_____

_____

_____

## Week 11 · Day 4

*He gave some to be apostles, some to be prophets, and some to be evangelists, pastors, and teachers. But the majority is not called to do that. The majority of us are called to work, to labor, and to reach the people in our sphere of influence.*

-JOHN BEVERE

In Romans 10 we see one of the most important principles in the gospel. "Whoever calls on the name of the LORD shall be saved" (v. 13) But we also read there, "How shall they believe in Him of whom they have not heard? And how shall they hear without a preacher? And how shall they preach unless they are sent?" (v. 14).

While each one of us is commissioned by God to be witnesses of the gospel, God has called some to be in full-time ministry. They go out and preach to reach the masses that need Christ. They also teach and train the saints (Eph. 4). But most of us are not called to be preachers in a full-time capacity.

If the majority are not called to preach full time, what are they called to do? And how can they reach the world for Christ? The answer is simple and inspiring. God commissioned and entrusted the greater part of His church with a different integral part. This includes working, making money or receiving wages, and reaching those within your circle of influence with the gospel. You will be able to reach your co-worker, your family, the check-out person you see each week at the grocery store, as well as those in your spheres of influence in ways your pastor (or other full-time ministers) never will.

And there is much more for those who understand this principle. Besides your calling to those around you, you can reach multitudes worldwide by *partnering* with those who are called to full-time ministry!

The Lord never intended full-time ministries to receive their necessary finances by the distribution of angels or by money falling from the sky. Rather, He entrusted His body with the privilege of giving, which creates a partnership. We saw in yesterday's devotion how partnerships multiply the effort of a single person or group into a powerful relationship that can accomplish nearly any goal.

Your tithe belongs in your local church, but you can partner with other ministries with offerings above your first 10 percent. As you consistently give to God-ordained ministries, you join with them as they touch others. When you stand before the Judgment Seat of Christ, you will not only be rewarded for the lives you personally affected, but also for the multitudes you reached and trained through partnering with God-ordained ministries.

Are you partnering in the gospel? If not, how can you begin? If you are already, how is your partnership affecting people through the ministries receiving your gift?

---
---
---
---
---

## Week 11 · Day 5

*You give what's temporal, but you convert it to the eternal in the process of partnership, and it's multiplied on top of that. Not only do you get a harvest of multiplication back on this earth so that you can do more, but you also have the partnership that is more important: your fruit, which is in heaven.*

-JOHN BEVERE

God is so good!

Now he who supplies seed to the sower and bread for food will also supply and increase your store of seed and will enlarge the harvest of your righteousness. You will be made rich in every way so that you can be generous on every occasion, and through us your generosity will result in thanksgiving to God.

-2 CORINTHIANS 9:10-11, NIV

Not only does God freely give seed to the sower (the sower is you and the seed is your life, talents, time, money and abilities, as well as the provisions you need every day), but He also multiplies your seed as you sow it back into His kingdom! He first gives to you, you give to Him, He gives you more again, and it continues in a cycle where you just can't out give God!

To top it all off, *even though it is all by Him and comes from Him in the first place*, He empowers us to increase it and then He rewards us for it, both now and eternally in heaven!

And there is another reason to bless God for His giving us the ability to partner with Him and each other. *Partnering gives you the opportunity to give back to the ministries that have touched your life!* In doing this, there is another miracle that takes place! It's your way of saying, "Thank You, Lord, for the ministry gift that you've sent me." This establishes a relationship with that ministry. God designed it like this on purpose, because the more people a ministry touches and reaches, the greater the financial needs become for them to operate.

They've touched more people, so more people say, "Thank you," by partnering with that ministry. That gives the ministry the ability to maintain a greater level of God's work. That's the way God ordained it, and He is the one who gives the increase.

Isn't this incredible how God works to bless all involved? What is the Holy Spirit saying to you now?

## Week 11 · Day 6

*Another way we can multiply is through prayer. We can eternally touch lives....by praying for individuals, families, churches, cities, and nations. We can also touch lives by praying for ministries.*

-JOHN BEVERE

Prayer is one of the ways we become intimate with God, and through our intimate knowledge of Him grace and peace are multiplied to us. Through the divine power of prayer we can also bless others. One of the greatest things about prayer is that it is not limited by time or space. You can pray for people you do not know personally, people you may never meet. Interestingly, legitimate scientific studies have even verified it.

"A randomized, controlled study published in the current issue of the American Medical Association's *Archives of Internal Medicine* shows empirically that "intercessory prayer produced a measurable improvement in the medical outcomes of critically ill patients."[1]

"In this study I have attempted to determine whether intercessory prayer...has any effect on the medical condition and recovery of hospitalized patients....these data suggest that intercessory prayer to the Judeo-Christian God has a beneficial therapeutic effect in patients admitted to a CCU."[2]

- RANDOLPH C. BYRD, MD, SAN FRANCISCO, CALIFORNIA

These only prove what we already know by faith and by experience.

Confess your trespasses to one another, and *pray for one another, that you may be healed. The effective, fervent prayer of a righteous man avails much.*

-JAMES 5: 16 (EMPHASIS ADDED)

Our righteousness is in Christ, and when we pray fervently in faith according to God's Word, our prayers avail much, producing amazing supernatural results.

God touches multitudes, multiplying the kingdom by our prayers when we pray for ministries' needs. Although financial partnership is very important to ministries so they can keep operating, prayer partnership is even more so! Ministries need your prayer on a regular basis – for finances, staff, wisdom, health, safety, outreach, and more. When you pray for a ministry, you will share in the eternal reward for every soul who is touched by them!

Are you partnered in prayer with your church and any other ministries? Ask the Lord whom you should be praying for.

1. "Major Study Proves Scientifically That Prayer Works," Kansas City, November 2, 1999, LifeSiteNews.com, http://www.life-site.net/ldn/1999/nov/99110204.html (accessed March 4, 2006).
2. Randolph C. Byrd, MD, "Positive Therapeutic Effects of Intercessory Prayer in a Coronary Care Unit Population," *Southern Medical Journal* 81 (July 1988): 826-829, http://www.godandscience.org/apologetics/smj1.html (accessed March 4, 2006).

## Week 11 · Day 7

*We share and share alike.
Those who go to the
battle and those who
guard the equipment.*

-KING DAVID,
IN 1 SAMUEL 30:24

The heroes of war are usually the soldiers who do exploits on the battlefield. But no army can effectively go to war without those at home who keep the supplies coming. The more support that is provided, the more effective those on the frontline can be. **As part of God's spiritual army, serving ministries is another way we multiply God's kingdom.** By serving, we mean contributing to the "spiritual war effort" with our time, talents, gifts, and abilities.

Some think, *Well, I'm not very talented. I can't do much. About all I can do is make lunch.* Don't short-change yourself like that. The humblest of gifts can be the most glorious. Hospitality, cooking good meals or baked goods are true talents. Ministry organizations need this kind of help all the time, and who knows how many you can bless as you work behind the scenes in the kitchen and at the table? Perhaps you never realized how many ways you could bless the Lord with those skills! Never underestimate ministries of support. Trying to run a church or ministry organization without these can mean the battle may be severely hindered regardless of how gifted those on the front lines are.

God designed us so that we need each other. As we consistently give what may seem small and insignificant, we will see how critical our contributions really are and how our seed is multiplied! *At the Judgment Seat, all a ministry touches is credited not just to the leaders, but also to all those who faithfully served, gave, and prayed, even if they were not on the scene of the battlefield.*

You have abilities and opportunities to serve in ways you may never have realized. Ask God to show you exactly how He desires you to get involved, so you too can share in the eternal rewards! And remember this as you serve:

An integral part of receiving rewards for your service is your attitude....It is not just our works that count, but the motives that fuel our works, and our attitude will affect our motives. God says, "If you are willing and obedient, you shall eat the good of the land" (Isa. 1:19).

-JOHN BEVERE

Outward appearance and inner attitude can be two different things. It's possible to look humble, submitted, and obedient on the outside – even impressing yourself – but in your heart and mind you have your own ideas about things. With your own agenda you become resentful, bitter, or full of envy or personal ambition. Pride and a rebellious, defiant attitude of heart may be the reality. Or maybe it's not so full blown, but is just a seed of occasional critical or picky gossip or envy.

We may be "only human," easily prone to poor attitudes and wrong motives. But for the believer, that is no excuse. Rather, it is exactly why we must walk in the Spirit and examine our hearts by the Word.

Assuming that you have really heard Him and been taught by Him, as [all] Truth is in Jesus [embodied and personified in Him], strip yourselves of your former

nature [put off and discard your old unrenewed self] which characterized your previous manner of life and becomes corrupt through lusts and desires that spring
from delusion; and be constantly renewed in the spirit of your mind [having a fresh
mental and spiritual attitude], and put on the new nature (the regenerate self) created in God's image, [Godlike] in true righteousness and holiness.
-EPHESIANS 4:21-24, AMP

If we will intimately follow Christ, He will give us the right attitude. But what do we do
when we behold ugly sin within our heart? We simply face it and repent of it! God will
change our attitudes if we seek Him and humble ourselves before Him.

Keeping a godly attitude in all you do is essential. Your attitude will affect your motives,
and at the Judgment Seat you will be rewarded not only for your works, but also for your
motives that fueled them.

*Driven by Eternity:*
## YOUR WEEK IN REVIEW

- God gives grace to the humble, and He is calling you to go for more grace
  in your life.

- ALL that we give to the Lord in faith is multiplied and will reap an
  eternal reward!

- Partnerships give everyone the ability to accomplish so much more
  than they could do alone.

- Choosing to enter into partnerships with godly ministries allows every
  person to reach multitudes throughout the world.

- When you pray for a ministry you share the eternal rewards of that
  ministry.

- Serving with our time, talents, gifts, and abilities is a way to multiply.

- Our motives will be judged, so we must seek to keep a godly attitude.

As we cultivate the grace of God in our lives, He gives us more, and we can sow into His
kingdom with our very best. To be great in God's world is to be servant of all. Let the Lord
encourage and enlighten you. He desires you to experience the deep satisfaction and warm
sense of community that comes when you feel truly useful, needed, and an important part
of the family of God!

How are you thinking and feeling right now? Are there abilities and skills you have that
you never really thought of as being useful, important or a blessing?

What is the Holy Spirit saying about how you can maximize your life for God by using and multiplying what He has already given you?

_____

_____

How's your attitude?

_____

_____

# Multiplying the Grace of God

**Going for grace!**

Grace and peace be multiplied to you in the knowledge of God and of Jesus our Lord.

-2 PETER 1:2

1.  God wants you to go for all the grace you can. How can you do that? Can you think of some Scripture verses to go along with your answer?

2.  In what ways are you going for more grace in your life right now?

3.  As the grace of God abounds in our lives, what does 2 Corinthians 9:9 have to say about our giving into the kingdom, and what does this have to do with the judgment?

    As it is written, He [the benevolent person] scatters abroad; He gives to the poor; His deeds of justice and goodness and kindness and benevolence will go on and endure forever!

    - 2 COR. 9:9 (AMP)

## Multiplication miracle!
Read this passage:

And [God] Who provides seed for the sower and bread for eating will also provide *and multiply* your [resources for] sowing *and increase* the fruits of your righteousness [which manifests itself in active goodness, kindness, and charity]. Thus you will be enriched in all things and in every way, so that you can be generous, and [your generosity as it is] administered by us will bring forth thanksgiving to God.

-2 CORINTHIANS 9:10-11 AMP, EMPHASIS ADDED

4.  Our lives, talents, abilities, resources – all we have – are likened to seeds and fruit. Where does all we have and all we can do come from in the first place?

5.  Once we give of our life, talents, abilities, skills, finances, and so on, there are several miraculous things that take place when we sow them according to God's will. What happens to the seeds when we are givers?

**One of the greatest ways we can multiply the grace of God in our lives is though giving.**
Second Corinthians 9:7 says, "God loves a cheerful giver." Our giving to others, especially those in need who can't repay us, brings rewards both now in this life and at the judgment.

6.  What are the three ways you can give to God and see the miracle of multiplication?

7.  What is a partnership, and what is so great about it?

## Ministry Partnership

 The majority of us are NOT called to go into full time ministry. What is your responsibility in reaching the world for Christ?

8. Describe the partnership between those who are called to full-time ministry and those who are not. (Do you recall what King David said about this?)

9. Partnership is definitely a way to say "thank you" to ministries that have blessed us. But it is also much more than that. Why is partnership so vital to a ministry's operations and growth?

10. Some who are wealthy give little; some who have little give much. When you give to God, what does God look at?

11. What would happen if all of us started multiplying our gifts, talents, skills, and finances through giving into the kingdom?

_____

_____

_____

_____

_____

When we give to God, not only does our giving grow eternally, but it also expands in the natural world. This gives us the ability to give more and reach even more people. It is a cycle that continually renews itself and increases.

## The Power of Your Prayer

There's nothing more powerful than praying according to the Word of God!

- Ministries need our prayer support. Pray from Philippians 4:6-7 "Lord, I pray for _____ (insert minister and/or ministry name here): that they are anxious for nothing, having no fear or anxiety, but in everything by prayer and supplication, with thanksgiving, they let their requests be made known to God; and I pray that the peace of God, which surpasses all understanding, will guard their hearts and minds through Christ Jesus."

- Many ministers travel throughout the world. There are many Scriptures about God's protection and care. Psalm 34:19-20 is just one you could pray, "Lord, You said many evils would confront the righteous. Lord, I pray for _____ (insert minister and/or ministry name here) that You would deliver him/her out of them all and that You keep all his/her bones; not one of them is broken. According to Your Word, Lord, I pray You will keep and protect _____ (insert minister and/or ministry name here) from harm, keeping them in your grace and safety."

Remember, every person a ministry touches, if you've partnered with that ministry, you will share in the reward!

## Multiplication Through Serving Ministries

You are very important to God's plans. And the Lord desires to prosper you! Many in the church never are blessed simply because they just "attend" church rather than becoming an active part of God's community! And it is so easy to be involved through humble acts of service. Countless people testify the little steps they took to get involved made for big blessings in their lives!

No great pressure, no super qualifications. If you can hand out a piece of paper, if you can smile, if you can point people in a direction – God has an important ministry for you! And it will have plenty of eternal rewards, because ministries need all kinds of help from people just like you!

12. How can YOU take responsibility for your part in God's kingdom? Ask the Lord for His will, wisdom, and direction.

_____

_____

_____

_____

_____

_____

_____

_____

The pressure is off; you don't have to do some big-time ministry to impact the world! Just enter into relationships with godly ministries through simple consistent acts of joyful giving and service!

> From him the whole body, joined and held together by every supporting ligament, grows and builds itself up in love, as each part does its work.
> -EPHESIANS 4:16, NIV

**No matter how insignificant your part seems, remember that every part is vital; you can be as effective or ineffective as you choose.**
God says, "If you are willing and obedient, you shall eat the good of the land" (Isa. 1:19). It is not just our service or outward works that count, but the motive which fuels our works. We are to be not only outwardly obedient but also truly willing in our hearts.

13. What is going to keep our motives pure?

_____

_____

_____

_____

_____

_____

_____

Having the right attitude is the key. We will either gain rewards or lose them, and it all depends on our attitude.

> _Look to yourselves that we do not lose those things we have worked for, but that we may receive a full reward._
> 2 John 8

**ZENITH**
the time when
something is
most powerful
or successful.

What is the main thing God has shown you about multiplying His grace in your life?

_____

_____

_____

_____

_____

_____

_____

_____

_____

_____

_____

_____

_____

_____

_____

_____

_____

_____

_____

_____

_____

_____

_____

_____

_____

_____

_____

_____

_____

_____

_____

_____

_____

_____

_____

_____

THE
ZENITH

HOUR

Please refer to Chapter 13,

Personal Influence,

in the *Driven by Eternity* book

and video session 12.

# Week 12 · Day 1

*I think there is no life as great as to see people who are lonely, insecure, fearful, unloved, uncared for, forgotten or neglected, and to be able to give them the message of God's big love-plan that helps them stand up and straighten their shoulders...realizing that they count with God. To lift people and to help them discover the rich and purposeful life God created them for, to help them discover that God loves them, that Jesus gave His life for them...that is the greatest life on earth.*

-T. L. OSBORN

We must take note that although Christ is above all, we never see Him talking down to people. On the contrary, He always brings dignity, forgiveness, and hope where He had the right to have brought shame and penalty for sin. Think of the woman taken in adultery, whom He forgave in front of the condemning crowd, or of Peter who denied Christ, but then was lovingly called to feed His sheep!

We must do the same. As new creations in Christ, we are to put on the new nature, following Jesus in His footsteps. He is our example – not a stressed-out, selfish, self-absorbed culture.

Tell the truth, in love, even if it hurts, yes. Confront sin, definitely. Speak plainly about the realities of life and death, heaven and hell, for sure. God and His people are not afraid to get dirt under their fingernails from the stuff of real life. That is what makes Jesus so amazing and authentic. Willingly He came among us, called us friends, brothers and sisters, little children and loved ones. Those are the words and realities of a God who came to tear down sin but uplift sinners, to give life and life abundantly.

It is important to make sure we view people as Christ views them – precious and all together lovely. We are cultivating a life of love by the Holy Spirit, keeping others' best interests in mind and acting accordingly.

God will judge our personal character. Great deeds and lofty accomplishments will crumble at the judgment if they are built on the foundation of self. But a foundation of God-filled character that esteems others more highly than ourselves will stand. Make no mistake about it: how we treat people in everyday life greatly reveals the character of our heart.

How about you? Have you viewed people through your own eyes or the eyes of Christ?

1. T. L. Osborn, *The Big Love Plan* (Tulsa, OK: OSFO Books, 1984), 115-116.

## Week 12 · Day 2

*If we value individuals, we will seek to build and strengthen their lives out of a heart of compassion and love. If we see people as sources, we'll use them.*

-JOHN BEVERE

A benchmark is a standard by which something can be measured or judged. How do we know if we are living properly? How can we be sure we are doing things the way God wants us to?

Thank God He has given us the true benchmark, the ultimate standard. And we can easily go to it daily to check our progress, make any necessary adjustments, be encouraged in our life, and keep fighting the good fight. Better still, this is not a dry, dead system of measurement, but a new and living way of life.

*The test for all we do is the Word of God.* The Scriptures are our perfect guide. As we intimately walk with the Lord by the power of the Holy Spirit we know we are His. We are empowered by His grace as we keep His Word. And the world too will know whom we serve when we live by God's standard for all to see.

What about the standard for how we are to treat others? For the Christian, there is no mystery. Among many other places in the Bible it is found in Philippians 2:3 (NIV):

Do nothing out of selfish ambition or vain conceit, but in humility consider others better than yourselves.

What a culture shock that verse is to those who live in the world, who are new to the faith, or who live according to the flesh. Society may not embrace this commandment of God, but the standard is clear, this call from God is for all of us. And if we will seek Him, He will empower us to fulfill it.

We are to be humble, regardless of title or position, wealth or power, education or status. We are to esteem others more highly than ourselves, not by constraint, but because the love of God for all people is in us.

Think on these things and pray. Do you compassionately seek to build up and strengthen others, valuing them above yourself?

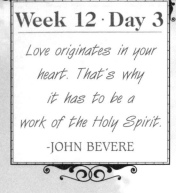

**Week 12 · Day 3**

*Love originates in your heart. That's why it has to be a work of the Holy Spirit.*

-JOHN BEVERE

The Bible tells us God is love. He doesn't have love, but His very nature is love. Jesus walked on this earth as the physical representation of love. Studying the way He lived would be wise for us. Living the way He did is true, godly wisdom.

We have many opportunities today to treat people out of revenge, selfishness, envy, or hatred. But we also have opportunities to love those who hate, curse, or mistreat us, as Luke 6:27-28 tells us. If our lives have been dedicated to following Christ and being His disciples, then our very hearts and thoughts should be driven by the love of Christ.

Many years ago a missionary followed his call to the Sudan. There he saw many horrible things as he ministered the gospel to the people there. At one point he was kidnapped, beaten, and left for dead in the desert. By the grace of God he was found and had the opportunity to recover. When asked what his next step would be, he responded with, "Return and share with them the love of Christ." His heart was to see the people saved, lives restored, and God's glory to reign where it was being overshadowed by darkness. He had a heart and a mind to love.

We may not be missionaries called to the Sudan, but wherever there is darkness reigning in our communities, we have the opportunity to bring love and "push back the darkness" by operating with and in the Spirit of God.

> Through you we push back our enemies, through your name we trample our foes.
> -PSALM 44:5, NIV

How can you be active in bringing light to dark situations in your community right now? What situations do you know that need the love of Christ where you can minister?

_____

_____

_____

_____

_____

_____

_____

_____

_____

_____

_____

## Week 12 · Day 4

*When we love...we will be full of hope and endure any hardship for the benefit of the kingdom or another's well-being. Bottom line, we will live for the godly edification of others, which is only found in their conformity to Christ in fulfilling His will in their lives.*

-JOHN BEVERE

Love is patient, love is kind. It does not envy, it does not boast, it is not proud. It is not rude, it is not self-seeking, it is not easily angered, it keeps no record of wrongs. Love does not delight in evil but rejoices with the truth. It always protects, always trusts, always hopes, always perseveres. *Love never fails.*

-1 CORINTHIANS 13:4-8, NIV, EMPHASIS ADDED

Written by a rugged, often maligned and beaten apostle Paul, the above Scripture was not mere philosophy or empty words. God's love was a way of life in his perilous travels, in front of powerful dignitaries, for peasants and pagans, in prison, in tortures, in the church. Paul lived the life and walked the talk, carrying an authority no one could really dispute – *the life of one who didn't just talk about love, but lived it.*

Look at his words in Romans 8:37-9:3 (emphasis added):

*Yet in all these things we are more than conquerors through Him who loved us.* For I am persuaded that neither death nor life, nor angels nor principalities nor powers, nor things present nor things to come, nor height nor depth, nor any other created thing, shall be able to separate us *from the love of God* which is in Christ Jesus our Lord. I tell the truth in Christ, *I am not lying*, my conscience also bearing me witness in the Holy Spirit, that I have great sorrow and continual grief in my heart. *For I could wish that I myself were accursed from Christ for my brethren*, my countrymen according to the flesh.

Paul's love became so great he desired to be cursed himself if it were possible that it would bring salvation for others! Only the love of God could bring a person to make that statement, as Paul himself declares.

Are you one who only talks about love, or do you *live* it?

# Week 12 · Day 5

*Some of the individuals who have impacted my life the most you're never going to see behind pulpits in this earth. Because they're not preachers.*

-JOHN BEVERE

How much of a difference can a humble servant make? How about *changing the world as we know it?*

In Acts 8 and 9 we hear of God's servant Ananias. One day the Lord called to Ananias, and his simple response, "I'm here, Lord," has had a major impact on all generations. God told Ananias in a vision to reach out to someone unexpected, someone most people would not reach out to, Saul of Tarsus. There was hardly a person in that day that didn't know of Saul as one who was persecuting, killing, and torturing Christians throughout the land. What Ananias didn't know was that Saul had just recently been blinded by God on the road to Damascus.

In one act of obedience, Ananias prays for Saul, and Saul receives his sight and becomes a believer and follower of Christ.

Look at what the *IVP Commentary* has to say about Saul, who then became the apostle we know as Paul:

The most important event in human history apart from the life, death and resurrection of Jesus of Nazareth is the conversion to Christianity of Saul of Tarsus. If Saul had remained a Jewish rabbi, we would be missing thirteen of twenty-seven books of the New Testament and Christianity's early major expansion to the Gentiles. Humanly speaking, without Paul Christianity would probably be of only antiquarian or arcane interest, like the Dead Sea Scrolls community or the Samaritans.

Although Ananias did not know the impact of his obedience, he was a man who consistently lived in obedience to God and changed the rest of Christianity. The Bible says he was a devout disciple. Love was his way of life.

Only God knows how many people are blessed because of a simple act of your obedience.

Have you seen miracles happen in your or someone else's life as a result of obedience to God?

## Week 12 · Day 6

*How you respond to a police officer, the way you speak of your pastor, the manner in which you conduct your financial affairs, the words you use to speak to individuals, and the list continues, these all affect the lives of others around you. Will you be a builder or a stumbling block?*

-JOHN BEVERE

Multitudes of people have no idea how important the "little things" are, or at very least they minimize them. Financial integrity, telling "little white lies," cheating in school or at work, dealing with our families and friends, lusts and envy, how we live at home where few people see us...just the impressively simple fact that the list is so extensive argues for how important the so-called "little things" are. And God has one of the most powerful verses in the entire Bible, tucked away in the always captivating Song of Solomon, to speak directly to us!

Catch us the foxes, the little foxes that spoil the vines, for our vines have tender grapes.
-SONG OF SOLOMON 2:15

If we had any real idea of what this verse means, we would change our very lives! You see, in the not too distant past (and in some areas of the world today) people might live or die depending on a good year from their crops. A good harvest is needed both to eat and to trade. In this example, all the hopes, the future...all the care and expense...all the nurturing, time, and effort could go into the vineyard, and then one little thing could happen to ruin it all! And if it did, it could destroy the entire harvest and bring destruction with it!

What little thing could do this? A whole family's livelihood, a great field of beauty and productivity could be wiped out by something as "cute" and "harmless" as...little foxes! If these animals of the field were allowed to chase prey and to frolic in the vineyards, they would trample the green shoots of the vines and ruin the crop! The more little foxes, the more crops destroyed. So the caretaker must be ever vigilant to not allow the "little things" to destroy the whole harvest!

You can readily see what God is trying to tell us. The "little foxes" represent our "small" sins, the things we do that grieve the Holy Spirit and threaten to ruin the whole harvest of our lives. Like the vineyard worker, we must not allow these little foxes to destroy the vine. We do this not through total self-discipline or self-mastery, but by the Spirit of God. In His power we can eradicate the "little sins" of compromise and self-indulgence that our flesh and unrenewed minds latch onto!

To live a life that bears a great harvest, realize the danger of the "little" sins is *not* so little!

Are there any "little foxes" you see spoiling your vines? Ask the Lord to help you deal with them in your life.

## Week 12 · Day 7

*If we only could realize
that while we are yet
mortals that day by
day we are building for
eternity. How different
our lives, in many ways,
would be. Every gentle
word, every generous
thought, every unselfish
deed will become a pillar
of eternal beauty in
the life to come.*

-REBECCA RUTER
SPRINGER

To be *driven by eternity* means every moment, everything, is seen in its light. The black darkness of self and sin is obliterated by the light of God's love.

> For you were once darkness, but now you are light in the Lord. Live as children of light (for the fruit of the light consists in all goodness, righteousness and truth) and find out what pleases the Lord.
>
> -EPHESIANS 5:8-10, NIV

Notice that the above passage doesn't say you were once "in" darkness. No, you *were* darkness and doomed to spend eternity *in* darkness. But "*now you are light in the Lord*"! Not just "in" the light, but you *are* light. And you are to live as a child of light, finding out what pleases the Lord.

Being driven by eternity is about pleasing the Lord. But we live in a dark, dark world. How are we to know how to please the Lord, and ultimately how do we find our way home to Him in eternity? *We must trust Him, obey Him, and look to Him; He will bring us home.* Psalm 43:3 (NIV) says, "Send forth your light and your truth, let them guide me; let them bring me to your holy mountain, to the place where you dwell."

*Driven by eternity* means driven by God's plans, God's calling, and God's purpose for your life. Anything else, anything less will burn at the judgment. How do we know that what we are doing, how we are living is according to God's will, His calling for our life?

> But whoever lives by the truth comes into the light, so that it may be seen plainly that what he has done has been done through God.
>
> -JOHN 3:21, NIV

Shouldn't we just "get real"? Isn't it too much to expect anyone to live like this? Aren't times just too difficult, people just too weak and overcome by the world? No, not at all. Not even close. The reality is that we are empowered by grace through the truth of God's Word and by the Holy Spirit, and God is moving mightily for those who live intimately with Him!

> Anyone who claims to be intimate with God ought to live the same kind of life Jesus lived. My dear friends, I'm not writing anything new here. *This is the oldest commandment in the book, and you've known it from day one.* It's always been implicit in the Message you've heard. On the other hand, perhaps it is new, freshly minted as it is in both Christ and you – *the darkness on its way out and the True Light already blazing!*
>
> -1 JOHN 2:6-8, THE MESSAGE, EMPHASIS ADDED

For those who will live driven by eternity, the True Light is already blazing! Eternity is now, to be lived for in this life. When we die, we go to our eternal destiny in heaven with the Lord.

As we close these twelve hours of devotions, let's look at one last thing, and then we will review.

> Let your light so shine before men, that they may see your good works and glorify your Father in heaven.
>
> -MATTHEW 5:16

Become a blazing light! Witness as you never have before! God is Light, and in Him is no darkness (1 John 1:5). *You* are the light of the world (Matt. 5:14)! Just let the Holy Spirit cause you to be driven by eternity, and your light will shine on darkness and God will give you the words, the things to do, the way to live as you tell others about the Light of your life!

> The fruit of the [uncompromisingly] righteous is a tree of life, and he who is wise captures human lives [for God, as a fisher of men – he gathers and receives them for eternity].
>
> -PROVERBS 11:30, AMP

Take the chance to reach out to others. Don't let fear keep you from telling others about Jesus, about eternity. The Apostle Pauls, the Billy Grahams of the world were ministered to by someone. You just don't know what God has planned for that person you know who needs the Lord.

A seed will multiply though it looks insignificant. Don't ever take the leading of the Holy Spirit for granted; don't ignore Him. The most insignificant things He leads you to do may turn out to be the most significant multiplication factors of your life – not to mention the salvation and destiny you bring to those you minister to. *God wants you to multiply. God also wants to reward you for your multiplication, as you are DRIVEN BY ETERNITY!*

### *Driven by Eternity:*
## YOUR WEEK IN REVIEW

- How you treat people in everyday life greatly reveals the character of your heart.
- You are to esteem others more highly than yourself.
- The love of God is shed abroad in your heart by the Holy Spirit, so you can love others.
- You are not just to talk about love or theorize about it, but to LIVE it.
- Only God knows how many people are blessed because of a simple act of your obedience.
- To live a life that bears a great harvest, realize that the danger of the "little" sins is *not* so little!
- God wants you to multiply. God also wants to reward you for your multiplication, as you are *DRIVEN BY ETERNITY!*

So much is at stake. Don't take your time on earth lightly. Both your and other people's eternal destinies are dependent upon your obedience to the plan of God. You can fulfill your calling and make your election sure by running your race fully to the end.

Think about it: *You'll look back ten million years from this moment and rejoice that you did.* How does that incredible statement make you feel? What is the Lord saying to you about it right now?

_____

_____

_____

_____

You cannot be too committed to the will of God. So run your race to win! **Take some time to do two things to sort it all out**, letting God send out His light and truth to lead you and guide you by His Word.

(NOTE: If you can't fit it all in now, set aside some more time later. The point is NOT to just be done with another study or set of devotions. **The point is to live *driven by eternity*, living each day with an eternal perspective.** Keep that your number one goal as you do these).

1. Sum up *your own* feelings, thoughts, and intentions from these devotions. If you want to, certainly you can go back and review your journaling and anything else you'd like. Let it all out, the struggles, the blessings, any questions and thoughts or words of encouragement.

   _____

   _____

   _____

   _____

2. Let the Lord speak to you; let *Him* sum up these devotions for you and for your life...what His feelings, thoughts, and intentions are for you. His plans for you are good, and He will make His will known to you day by day. Seek Him now, and you will be blessed with the fruit of your intimacy with Him!

   _____

   _____

   _____

   _____

May the Lord make your love for one another and for all people grow more and more and become as great as our love for you. In this way he will strengthen you, and you will be perfect and holy in the presence of our God and Father when our Lord Jesus comes with all who belong to him.

-1 THESSALONIANS 3:12-13, TEV

1. *My Dream of Heaven: A Nineteenth-Century Spiritual Classic*, originally known as *Intra Muros* (Cincinnati, OH: Harrison House, n.d.), 21.

# YOUR PERSONAL INFLUENCE

"And you shall love the LORD your God with all your heart, with all your soul, with all your mind, and with all your strength." This is the first commandment. And the second, like it, is this: "You shall love your neighbor as yourself." There is no other commandment greater than these.

-MARK 12:30-31

Our personal influence – how we treat people – and leading others to Jesus are two ways to multiply the grace of God in our lives. And we will be judged for these as well.

**The Basics of a Life** *Driven by Eternity*
You, then, why do you judge your brother? Or why do you look down on your brother? For we will all stand before God's judgment seat.

-ROMANS 14:10, NIV

1.  Why is how we treat others important to God?

2.  Why did Paul closely link the Judgment Seat to our attitude toward and treatment of others?

3.  How does our treatment of others *really* reveal our hearts?

**Will you be a builder or a stumbling block?** In making the life decision to be driven by eternity, you are declaring you will love others more than yourself.

4.  What is the Lord saying to *you* about the manner in which you conduct your financial affairs, how you act at work, the words you use to speak to individuals, and so on?

_____

_____

_____

---

**hot TOPIC**  Paul says it all in 2 Timothy 3:10 (NIV), *"You, however, know all about* my teaching, my way of life, my purpose, faith, patience, love, endurance..."* Can the same be said of you?

- Do the people you love, work with, come in contact with during the day, "know all about your teaching"? Have you told them about *the teachings* you know and live by?
- Do people know your *way of life*? That you live like a follower of Christ?
- Do they know *your purpose* is to love God *and* to love them?
- Have they heard of your faith, your patience, love and endurance through good times and not-so-good times? Have they seen God glorified in these?

Those are traits of a life driven by eternity. What is the Spirit saying to you about these in *your* life?

_____

_____

_____

---

**The greatest is the servant of all.**

In A.D. 56, the apostle Paul said, *"I am the least of all the apostles."* Seven years later, in A.D. 63, he wrote to the Ephesians and said, *"To me who am less than the least of all the saints."* And then right before he was beheaded, in A.D. 65, he wrote a letter to Timothy saying, *"Christ Jesus came into the world to save sinners, of whom I am chief."*

5.  If Paul was such a great apostle, what would explain his self-proclaimed seeming regression to the bottom of the barrel of all humanity?

_____

_____

6.  How is Paul's attitude in this one that is driven by eternity?

_____

_____

7.  How does Paul's worldview here differ from that of most people today?

_____

_____

**Your own worst enemy?**

    8.   The only one who can destroy the call of God on your life is you! How can that be?

_____

_____

**From the heart**

If I speak with human eloquence and angelic ecstasy but don't love, I'm nothing but the creaking of a rusty gate. If I speak God's Word with power, revealing all his mysteries and making everything plain as day, and if I have faith that says to a mountain, "Jump," and it jumps, but I don't love, I'm nothing. If I give everything I own to the poor and even go to the stake to be burned as a martyr, but I don't love, I've gotten nowhere. So, no matter what I say, what I believe, and what I do, I'm bankrupt without love.

-1 CORINTHIANS 13:1-3, THE MESSAGE

    9.   What are the three levels of communication, from lowest to highest?
The lowest level of communication is _____.
Why? Can you think of some Scriptures that show this?

_____

_____

_____

The next level of communication is _____.
Why? Can you think of some Scriptures that show this?

_____

_____

_____

The highest level of communication is that of the _____.
Why? Can you think of some Scriptures that show this?

_____

_____

_____

**The mighty power of worship!**

To get more of the love of God in your heart, you can cry out to God and ask for it. Often the most powerful prayers are the simplest, such as "Help, Lord" or "God, I need more of Your love in my heart." Praying for more grace, a lot of love, and a lot of the fear of the Lord will multiply the grace of God in your life.

Worshiping and praising God in prayer and song is also a mighty way to increase God's love in your heart and toward others. The few lines from the beautiful hymn below ask for the love of God to pulse in every beat of our hearts and cause us to be eternity-minded, not worldly-minded.

Read the words, and then spend a few moments in worship in your heart. As you worship, ask God to give you a few lines of your own "hymn." It doesn't need a melody (but it's fine if you have one), and it doesn't need to be a perfect rhyme or immensely profound or eloquent. Just let it be your heartfelt words of worship and supplication to God. Tell Him and ask Him whatever is on your heart as you write.

> **Spirit of God, Descend Upon My Heart**
> Spirit of God, descend upon my heart;
> Wean it from earth; through all its pulses move;
> Stoop to my weakness, mighty as Thou art;
> And make me love Thee as I ought to love.
> Hast Thou not bid me love Thee, God and King?
> All, all Thine own, soul, heart and strength and mind.
> I see Thy cross; there teach my heart to cling:
> O let me seek Thee, and O let me find!
> Teach me to love Thee as Thine angels love,
> One holy passion filling all my frame;
> The kindling of the heaven descended Dove,
> My heart an altar, and Thy love the flame.[1]

Now write your own as the Holy Spirit moves on your heart:

## "If it weren't for Charlie, I wouldn't be where I am today."

This video session had great stories of humble believers, whose names most people have never heard but their influence began with loving and reaching out to *one* person, and then multiplying into millions of people being touched. Charlie the janitor's influence has touched the thousands to whom Mike the accountant has ministered. Also, his influence has touched John Bevere through Mike. So the millions John has had the privilege to minister to have all been touched indirectly through Charlie as well.

Do you see how one janitor multiplied his seed and will one day be rewarded greatly? These men – Charlie, Mike, and the thrilling account of Jonathan Edwards – have affected innumerable lives. Their influence led to great legacies. *Yet it wasn't their public ministry that impacted these multitudes we speak of, but their personal lives. This is the privilege God gives everyone of us.*

The point is not that you need to be some great minister and touch millions of lives. This is not something you "work up"; it is the God-life you will naturally *live* when you decide to be *driven by eternity!* Charlie the janitor never knew the millions he would reach because of Mike who reached out to John Bevere. And Jonathan Edwards had long passed away before his real impact was realized! *But each of these understood that it is God who works in us, and living the gospel and esteeming others daily above ourselves will naturally bring forth multiplication, now and especially for eternity!*

10. Who was the person or persons that reached out to you, who may have been a Charlie or Mike in your life?

_____

11. How did this person(s) impact you? Did they go out of their way for you? What was it they did that brought you nearer to God?

_____

_____

Our lives have a "domino effect," or are like links in a chain. Tell a story of how you reached out to someone *and how that can be specifically related back to the person(s)* who first reached out to you.

_____

_____

Have you allowed the legacy to continue? Perhaps you've expressed your gratitude to those who first blessed you, or maybe you never got the opportunity or it was a stranger you didn't really know. But the greatest thanks you can give is to continue the ministry they gave you.

12. Can you think of any one person or group you have reached out to or sown seed into (a friend, an acquaintance, a ministry) to multiply the grace you've been given? Have they then touched others as well?

_____

_____

> The fruit of the [uncompromisingly] righteous is a tree of life, and he who is wise captures human lives [for God, as a fisher of men – he gathers and receives them for eternity].
>
> -PROVERBS 11:30, AMP

We can hear all these great things and tend to get worked up emotionally, running around and becoming more active in our own strength. But remember, we can't build anything except by the grace of God. So let's become more dependent on the Holy Spirit, asking Him for opportunities to be able to minister and to influence people's lives. As you do He will open up the doors. And as you're faithful, He will give you more and more because His will for your life is to multiply.

Write your own prayer here – and *really dig deep* – asking God...
- For His Spirit's leading in witnessing to others.
- For where and how to meet needs, giving as He directs you.
- To seal within your heart all you've learned in *Driven by Eternity*.

Use Scripture references in your prayer as they come to mind, and if the Lord brings up names of people or ways to minister or give, consider writing those down. **Let this be your personal prayer as you reach the zenith of Driven by Eternity!**

_____

_____

_____

_____

_____

_____

_____

_____

_____

**ZENITH**
the time when something is most powerful or successful.

God has entrusted you with great things! Never lose your passion, be discouraged, or think your part is insignificant. Others in your generation are counting on you, and your eternal destiny awaits you. You can succeed by utterly depending on His grace. He is faithful!

What is the *one thing* that most stood out to you in all of *Driven by Eternity*? What would the Lord have you do about it?

_____

_____

_____

_____

_____

_____

_____

_____

_____

## A Final Word

I appeal to you as a fellow citizen of the kingdom. Fulfill your calling and make your election sure; run your race fully to the end. You will look back ten million years from this moment and rejoice that you did. You cannot be too committed to the will of God. So run your race to win! As final words of encouragement, I leave you with one of Paul's earnest prayers for all the saints: *May the Lord make your love for one another and for all people grow more and more and become as great as our love for you. In this way he will strengthen you, and you will be perfect and holy in the presence of our God and Father when our Lord Jesus comes with all who belong to him* (1 Thess. 3:12-13, TEV).

-JOHN BEVERE

---

1. "Spirit of God, Descend Upon My Heart," by George Croly. Public domain.

We hope *Driven By Eternity* has helped you as you continue
on the life-long adventure available to those who make the decision
to live each day in obedience to God.

## Giving God glory...

If there is a personal story you would like to share about how this
curriculum has strengthened your relationship with God,
we would love to hear from you.
**mail@messengerintl.org**

## Other curriculums that will encourage your walk with God:

The Bait of Satan

Drawing Near

Fight Like a Girl

A Heart Ablaze

Kissed the Girls and Made them Cry

Under Cover

**www.messengerintl.org**

# APPENDIX A
## OUR NEED FOR A SAVIOR

There are two standards for living; one set by society and one set by God. Our culture may deem you "good" according to its parameters, but what does God think? Scripture tells us every person has fallen short of God's standard of right: "As the Scriptures say: 'There is no one who always does what is right, not even one.'" (Rom. 3:10 NCV) and again, "For all have sinned; all fall short of God's glorious standard." (Rom. 3:23 NLT)

To sin means to miss the mark of God's standard. Man was not created to be a sinner; rather Adam chose this course of his own free will. God placed the first man, Adam, in a beautiful world without sickness, disease, poverty, or natural disasters. There was no fear, hatred, strife, jealousy, and so forth. God called this place Eden, the very garden of God.

Adam chose to disobey God's command and experienced an immediate spiritual death, even though he did not die physically until hundreds of years later. Darkness entered his heart, and this spiritual death differs from physical death because in physical death the body ceases to exist; however, spiritual death is best described as separation from God, the very giver and source of all life.

Sin had entered Adam's makeup, and he fathered children after this nature: "And Adam lived one hundred and thirty years, and begot a son in his own likeness, after his image" (Gen. 5:3).

As a father his offspring were born after his nature and from this point forward each and every human is born into the image of his sin through their parents. Adam gave himself and his descendants over to a new lord, Satan, and with this captivity the natural world followed suit. A cruel lord now had legal claim to God's beloved creation. This is made clear in the following verses: "Then the devil, taking Him [Jesus] up on a high mountain, showed Him all the kingdoms of the world in a moment of time. And the devil said to Him, 'All this authority I will give to you, and their glory; for this has been delivered to me, and I give it to whomever I wish'" (Luke 4:5-6, author's emphasis).

Notice it was delivered to him. When? The answer is in the garden, for God originally gave the dominion of earth to man (see Gen. 1:26-28). Adam lost it all...this included himself and his seed for all generations. Again we read, "The whole world lies under the sway of the wicked one" (1 John 5:19).

Before God sent Adam from the garden, He made a promise. A deliverer would arise and destroy the bondage and captivity mankind had been subjected to.

This deliverer was born four thousand years later to a virgin named Mary. She had to be a virgin, as the father of Jesus was the Holy Spirit who impregnated her. If Jesus had been born to natural parents, He would have been born into the captivity of Adam.

He was Fathered by God and His mother was human. This made Him completely God and completely man. It had to be a son of man, who would purchase our freedom. For this reason Jesus constantly referred to Himself as the "Son of man." Though He was with the Father from the beginning, He stripped Himself of His divine privileges and became a man in order to give Himself as an offering for sin.

When He went to the cross, He took the judgment of our sin on Himself to free us from our bondage. Scripture declares, "He personally carried away our sins in his own body on the cross so we can be dead to sin and live for what is right." (1 Peter 2:24, NLT)

It's amazing: man sinned against God, and yet God (manifest in the flesh) paid the price for man's grave err. We read again, "For God made Christ, who never sinned, to be the offering for our sin, so that we could be made right with God through Christ." (2 Cor. 5:20-21, NLT)

Notice it says we could be made right. We do not receive the freedom which He paid so great a price for until we believe in our hearts that He died for us and was raised from the dead, and receive Him as our Lord; that is when He becomes our personal Savior. As Scripture states, "But to all who believed him and accepted him, he gave the right to become children of God. They are reborn! This is not a physical birth resulting from human passion or plan - this rebirth comes from God." (John 1:12-13, NLT)

When we receive Jesus Christ as our personal Lord and Savior, we die and are spiritually reborn. We die as slaves in the kingdom of Satan and are born as brand new children of God in His kingdom. How does this happen? Simple, when we believe this in our heart all we have to do is confess with our mouth Jesus as our Lord, and we are born again. Scripture affirms this: "For if you confess with your mouth that

Jesus is Lord and believe in your heart that God raised him from the dead, you will be saved. For it is by believing in your heart that you are made right with God, and it is by confessing with your mouth that you are saved." (Rom. 10:9-10, NLT)

It's that simple! We are not saved by our good deeds. Our good deeds could never earn us a place in His Kingdom. For if that was true, Christ died in vain. We are saved by His grace. It is a free gift that we cannot earn. All we have to do to receive is to renounce living for ourselves and commit our life to Him as Lord, which means Supreme Master. "He died for all, that those who live should live no longer for themselves, but for Him who died for them and rose again." (2 Cor. 5:15)

So if you believe Christ died for you, and you are willing to give Him your life and no longer live for yourself; then we can pray this prayer together and you will become a child of God:

God in Heaven, I acknowledge that I am a sinner and have fallen short of Your righteous standard. I deserve to be judged for eternity for my sin. Thank You for not leaving me in this state, for I believe you sent Jesus Christ, Your only begotten Son, who was born of the Virgin Mary, to die for me and carry my judgment on the Cross. I believe He was raised again on the third day and is now seated at Your right hand as my Lord and Savior. So on this day of _____, 20__, I give my life entirely to the Lordship of Jesus.

Jesus, I confess you as my Lord and Savior. Come into my life through Your Spirit and change me into a child of God. I renounce the things of darkness which I once held on to, and from this day forward I will no longer live for myself, but for You who gave Yourself for me that I may live forever.

Thank You Lord; my life is now completely in Your hands and heart, and according to Your Word I shall never be ashamed.

Now, you are saved; you are a child of God. All heaven is rejoicing with you at this very moment! Welcome to the family!

# APPENDIX B
## HOW TO BE FILLED WITH THE HOLY SPIRIT

Receiving the fullness of the Holy Spirit is as easy as receiving Jesus as your Lord and Savior. Some struggle, become discouraged, and can't receive most often due to the neglect of receiving basic scriptural instructions before asking. I've learned it is always best to show seekers what God says before praying, as this develops their faith to receive. So before I lead you in a prayer to receive, allow me first to instruct.

First and foremost, you must have already received Jesus Christ as your personal Lord and Savior (see John 14:17).

There can be no pattern of disobedience in your life. We are told that God gives His Spirit "to those who obey Him" (Acts 5:32). I've learned from experience this especially includes the area of unforgiveness. In our meetings I've seen many times hundreds receive the Holy Spirit and immediately speak in other tongues, yet a dozen or two of the hundreds stand and look bewildered. In almost every case in going to those few dozen I would find the Lord leading me to deal with harbored offense. Once the seekers forgave they immediately received and spoke in tongues. So before we go any further let's pray together.

Father, I ask that you would search me and show me if there is any disobedience in my heart. Please show me if there is any person I have withheld forgiveness from. I purpose to obey and forgive no matter what You reveal to me. I ask this in the name of Jesus and thank You so very much.

To receive the Holy Spirit all you have to do is ask! Jesus simply says, "If a son asks for bread from any father among you, will he give him a stone? Or if he asks for a fish, will he give him a serpent instead of a fish? Or if he asks for an egg, will he offer him a scorpion? If you then, being evil, know how to give good gifts to your children, how much more will your heavenly Father give the Holy Spirit to those who ask Him!" (Luke 11:11-13). He is simply saying that if our children ask us for something which is our will to give them, we won't give them something evil or different. In the same way, if you ask the Father for His Spirit, He won't give you an evil spirit. All you have to do is ask the Father in Jesus' name, and you will receive His Holy Spirit.

You must ask in faith. The New Testament tell us it is impossible to receive from God without faith. James 1:6-7 states: "But let him ask in faith, with no doubting, for he who doubts is like a wave of the sea driven and tossed by the wind. For let not that man suppose that he will receive anything from the Lord. So ask yourself at this moment, "When will I receive? Will it be when I speak in other tongues, or will it be the moment I ask?" Your answer should be - the moment you ask! For in the Kingdom, we believe then receive. Those who do not have faith say, "Show me and I will believe" but Jesus says, "I say to you, whatever things you ask when you pray, believe that you receive them, and you will have them" (Mark 11:24). Notice you believe first, and then you will have what you've asked for.

Acts 2:4 says, "And they were all filled with the Holy Spirit and began to speak with other tongues, as the Spirit gave them utterance." Notice they spoke with tongues; it was not the Holy Spirit who spoke in tongues. They had to do it, as the Spirit gave them the words. So there is a yielding! I can be in a swift moving river, but if I don't pick up my feet and yield to the river, I won't flow with it. So there are three areas we must yield: First, our lips. If I don't move my lips, words, whether in English or in a Foreign language, a heavenly tongue cannot come forth. Second, our tongue. If I don't move my tongue, I cannot speak. Third, our vocal chords. If I don't yield my vocal cords to my lungs, then I cannot speak.

You may at this point think I'm being sarcastic, but I'm not. After years of seeing people struggle, I've learned many subconsciously think the Holy Spirit is going to grab ahold of their lips, tongues, and vocal cords and make them speak. No, we speak, or yield, as He gives the utterance.

Jesus says, "'He who believes in Me, as the Scripture has said, out of his heart will flow rivers of living water.' But this He spoke concerning the Spirit, whom those believing in Him would receive; for the Holy Spirit was not yet given, because Jesus was not yet glorified" (John 7:38-39). When you ask for the Holy Spirit, you may have a syllable bubbling up, or rolling around in your head. If you will speak it in faith, it will be as if you open a dam, and the language will come forth. I like to see it as a spool of thread in your gut and the tip, or beginning of the thread, is glimpsed at your tongue, but as you begin to pull (speak), out comes the rest of the thread. Some think they are going to have the entire language in their mind then they will speak. No, we are to speak in faith.

I remember when my wife prayed to receive the Holy Spirit she didn't speak in tongues for a time, then she and a few friends were praying a few weeks later and she began to speak in tongues. She then said, "I had that syllable running through my head the past few weeks while praying, but didn't yield to it till tonight." I believe this is the case for so many - they ask, receive, but don't yield.

Scripture states, "The spirits of the prophets [spokespersons] are subject to the prophets" (1 Cor 14:32). This simply tells us that we are the ones who speak, and that the Holy Spirit will not force Himself on us. I recall the day after I was filled with the Holy Spirit I didn't know how to speak again. I went to another brother at the gym and asked, "How can I do it again?" He said, "John, you just do it!" I went out for a run and began to speak in tongues again while running. I was overcome with joy. We must remember the Holy Spirit is always ready to go; we are the ones who must yield. It is like a water fountain. The water is always there; all you have to do is turn the knob and out comes the water. So pray in tongues frequently!

Now that you have received basic instructions from the Scripture, if you believe you will receive we can pray together. One last thing: you cannot speak English and Spanish at the same time. Even so you can't speak in English and tongues at the same time. So remember, just believe and yield! Let's pray:

Father, in the name of Jesus, I come to you as Your child. You said if I asked You for the Holy Spirit You would give Him to me. With joy I now ask in faith; please baptize and fill me at this very moment with Your Holy Spirit. I receive all You have for me including the ability to speak in tongues. So now in faith I will speak in new tongues! Amen!

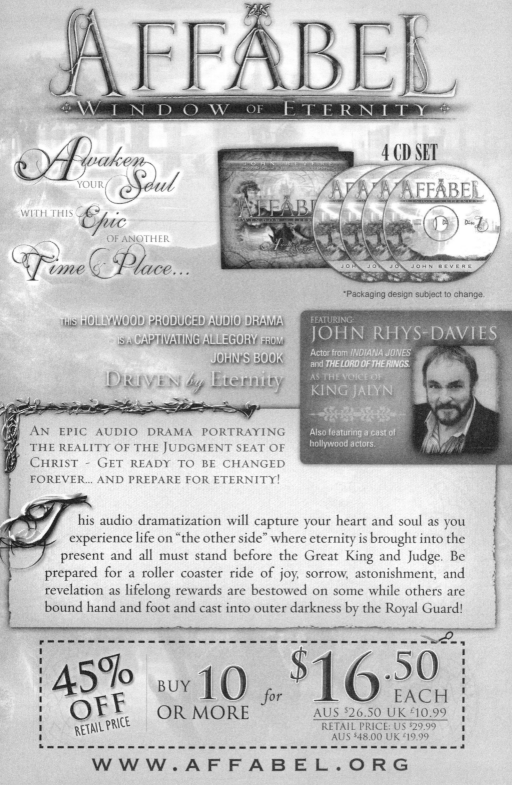

279

# MESSENGER INTERNATIONAL

*"Life-Transforming Truth"*

## BOOKS BY JOHN

*The Bait of Satan
Breaking Intimidation
The Devil's Door
*Drawing Near
*Driven by Eternity
The Fear of the Lord

*A Heart Ablaze
How to Respond when you Feel Mistreated
Thus Saith the Lord
*Under Cover
Victory in the Wilderness
Voice of One Crying

*Also available in curriculum

**Contact our ministry for a free 32-page color catalog and newsletter.**

The vision of MI is to strengthen believers, awaken the lost and captive in the church and proclaim the knowledge of His glory to the nations. John and Lisa are reaching millions of people each year through television and by ministering at churches, bible schools and conferences around the world. We long to see God's Word in the hands of leaders and hungry believers in every part of the earth.

**UNITED STATES**
PO Box 888
Palmer Lake, CO 80133-0888
**800-648-1477 (US & Canada)**
Tel: 719-487-3000
Fax: 719-487-3300
E-mail: mail@messengerintl.org

**EUROPE**
PO Box 622
Newport, NP19 8ZJ
UNITED KINGDOM
**Tel: 44 (0) 870-745-5790**
Fax: 44 (0) 870-745-5791
E-mail: europe@messengerintl.org

**AUSTRALIA**
PO Box 6200
Dural, D.C. NSW 2158
AUSTRALIA
In AUS 1-300-650-577
**Tel: +61 2 8850 1725**
Fax +61 2 8850 1735
Email: australia@messengerintl.org

The *Messenger* television program broadcasts in 216 countries on
GOD TV, the Australian Christian Channel and on the
New Life Channel in Russia. Please check your local listings for day and time.

## WWW.MESSENGERINTL.ORG